MASTER PAINTERS

LEONARDO

THE COMPLETE WORKS

AGNESE ANTONINI AND ALESSANDRO GUASTI

BARNES & NOBLE

NEW YORK

Contents

Chapter 1

Origins in the Florence of Lorenzo the Magnificent 4

Chapter 2

In Milan at the Court of Ludovico il Moro 48

Chapter 3

Commissions at the Time of the Florentine Republic 96

Chapter 4

The Final Years: Between Milan, Rome, and France 130

Chapter 5

The Myth of Leonardo 166

Index 186

Further Reading 190

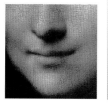

Chapter 1
Origins in the Florence of Lorenzo the Magnificent

T he scene is Vinci, a little village between Florence and Pisa, on the night of Saturday, April 15, 1452, at the third hour after nineteen o'clock—more or less our 10:00 p.m. An illegitimate boy is born to the twenty-five-year-old notary Ser (the honorable) Piero di Antonio da Vinci and the even younger Caterina, possibly a servant in his family, who will soon be married to one Antonio di Piero Buti del Vacca. Despite the fact that Ser Piero belongs to one of the most prominent families in the town, the lack of a wedding between the two young people causes no scandal; on the contrary, the presence of five godfathers and as many godmothers at the child's baptism attests to the acknowledged importance of the event. Everything is noted precisely by one grandfather, Antonio da Vinci: the hour, the day, and above all the name of the grandchild. "He had the name Lionardo. Baptizing priest Piero di Bartolomeo da Vinci. . . . "

Thus, the Tuscan hills were host to the infancy and early adolescence of Leonardo. Although he was illegitimate, he was unhesitatingly acknowledged by his father, who took him to live in the family home, while his natural mother went to live with her new husband on a farm owned by the da Vinci family at Anchiano. Not many months later, Leonardo acquired a young stepmother of sixteen, Albiera degli Amadori, descendent of a rich family originally from Florence. This was the first of Ser Piero's several marriages: After this first wife died in childbirth in 1464, there followed Francesca, daughter of Ser Giuliano Lanfredini, who in turn died in 1473. Taking her place was Margherita di Francesco di Jacopo, with whom Ser Piero had six children; seven more were the fruit of his union with Lucrezia di Guglielmo Cortigiani in 1485.

There are few records of Leonardo's first fifteen years in Vinci; he himself rarely mentioned this time in his own writings. But perhaps it is sufficient to picture the daily reality and dynamics of life in that little rural village in order to imagine what might most attract the eyes and the mind of a young genius. Leonardo's family owned farms, a mill, and a bakery, so his early years were passed in close contact with nature and with the bucolic life. This no doubt stimulated his probably innate propensity to observe the material world and to consider the value of lived experience. There were many opportunities to see and

Leonardo da Vinci
The Annunciation (detail)
1472–1475
Tempera and oil on canvas
38.58 x 85.43 inches
(98 x 217 cm)
Uffizi Gallery, Florence

make an idea become concrete in such a setting, and all this served to enrich his passion for experimentation, which soon expanded to more varied fields of study. This prompted him to turn his attention, methodically, to the investigation of natural phenomena and of the psychological realm—what he was later to call the "motions of the mind" that inspire every human act. Experience was his first teacher, and the fact that he did not study Latin and Greek, at that time considered indispensable for a person's cultural development, led him to call himself "an unlettered man." Nevertheless Vinci, although a rural village, was not entirely isolated from the issues that stirred the nearby cities: Pistoia, Empoli, Pisa, Florence were not so distant, even at that time; Ser Piero often went to Florence for work, just as other Florentine families had business dealings in the smaller town. Florence in the fifteenth century was characterized by a cultural ferment that echoed through all Tuscany, of which it was the political and economic center; this was probably what drew the da Vinci family to move there in 1468. Leonardo's grandfather, Antonio di Piero di Guido da Vinci, died that year, and soon after, his sixteen-year-old grandson, together with his father, left the place of his birth for Florence.

The young man's talent did not go unnoticed, even at this early point. A document of that year, discovered in the 1800s, mentions him. This is the *Cronaca rimata* (*Rhymed Chronicle*) of Giovanni Santi, father of the painter Raphael, in which he tells of a trip taken by Federico da Montefeltro, Duke of Urbino, to Milan in 1468, with stops in various places along the way. In speaking of Florence, the author pauses to mention the city's most outstanding artists and its emerging young ones: "Two youths equal in age and in loves / Leonardo da Vinci and the Perugian Pier della Pieve [Piero Perugino] who is a divine painter."

In Florence, Leonardo's father became notary to the ruling family, the Medici. A document dated 1469 refers to Ser Piero and his brother Francesco renting a house owned by the Arte dei Mercanti, one of the many civic guilds, in Via delle Prestanze (now Via dei Gondi). Leonardo was then still an only child, since Piero's first legitimate child wasn't born until 1476, to his third wife. That same year Leonardo is thought to have entered the workshop of Andrea del Verrocchio, one of the greatest Florentine artists of the fifteenth century. Giorgio Vasari, often acknowledged as the first art historian, wrote a biography of Leonardo in his *Le Vite delle più eccellenti pittori, scultori, ed architettori* (*Lives of the Most Excellent Painters, Sculptors, and Architects*), first published in its entirety in 1568. He recorded that Leonardo's father, observing his son's first drawings and evaluating the precocious talent they displayed, decided one day to take a few of them to be judged by Verrocchio, a close friend. Ser Piero was interested in learning what profit Leonardo might gain from dedicating himself

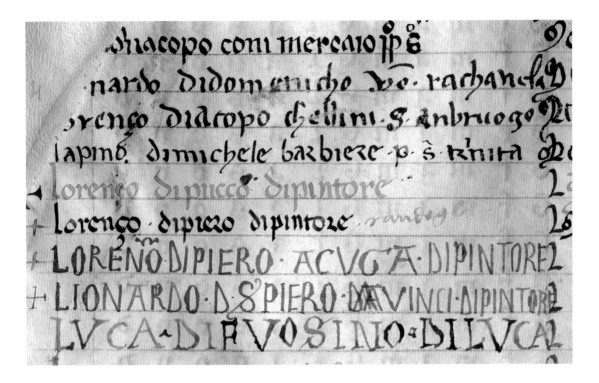

full time to the study of drawing and art. Vasari wrote, "Ser Piero . . . one day took some of his drawings and carried them to Andrea del Verrocchio, who was much his friend, and besought him straitly to tell him whether Leonardo, by devoting himself to drawing, would make any proficience. Andrea was astonished to see the extraordinary beginnings of Leonardo, and urged Ser Piero that he should make him study it; wherefore he arranged with Leonardo that he should enter the workshop of Andrea, which Leonardo did with the greatest willingness in the world."

Thus Leonardo entered the studio of Verrocchio. In the Renaissance, such a workshop provided a complete artistic education—necessary if one wished later to join a guild, or artist's union. The Renaissance workshop was a sort of "polyvalent laboratory" in which work was organized so that every member had to be skilled in all areas. According to the *Chronicles* of Benedetto Dei, around 1472 Florence was home to about forty painters' workshops, as many for goldsmiths and engravers, and more than eighty for woodworkers. These had the job of producing decorative objects of every sort, from paintings and sculptures to miniatures, jewelry, and objects for everyday use. A new apprentice normally would enter in early youth, at around ten years of age. Initially, the apprentice

Above:
From the register of the
Accademia di San Luca,
**Registration with
the name of
Leonardo da Vinci**
State Archives, Florence

Following pages:
Leonardo da Vinci
**Sketch of the
Arno Valley**
1473
Pen and ink on paper
Department of
Prints and Drawings,
Uffizi Gallery, Florence

would be given the most basic tasks, such as, in the case of painting, cleaning brushes, grinding pigments, and preparing the surfaces of the wood panels or canvases for painting. Then one would begin to draw, using silverpoint or pen and tempera on white or colored paper. The aim was to make young students learn all the skills necessary so that later they would be able to work alongside the master in completing his big commissions. From drawing as an exercise in itself one passed to the task of transferring preparatory drawings onto the painting support, which in itself was a fairly simple process. The next step was to paint the less important parts of a picture (clothing, backgrounds, secondary figures) in order to gain greater confidence and ability. In general, training was interdisciplinary, regardless of what kind of workshop one was in, involving drawing, painting, engraving, sculpture, and metalwork, so as to guarantee that the future artists would have versatile skills.

Entering the "laboratory" of Verrocchio, then, was Leonardo's opportunity to learn many different skills, since his master was himself talented in many disciplines, including metalwork, painting, and sculpture. In Verrocchio's workshop the students also studied optics, botany, and music, which satisfied the young artist's aforementioned propensity to investigate every aspect of nature. In these years of his development in Verrocchio's workshop Leonardo concentrated on drawing, especially on honing the precision of his depictions, following in the footsteps of the prior generation of artists, who had chosen painting as the most faithful means of reproducing reality. Whatever the instruction, whether in painting, metalwork, or sculpture, the young Leonardo absorbed it through work, as was the typical workshop practice. This permitted him to grapple with a range of technical problems and to test solutions one by one. He was learning under the guidance of one of the greatest sculptors of the age, but also through contact with other young students in that crucible of artists. Together Verrocchio's assistants represented the diamond points of Florentine art in the second half of the fifteenth century: Domenico Ghirlandaio, Sandro Botticelli, Piero Perugino, and Lorenzo di Credi were all apprentices in his workshop at this time. As their individual artistic vocabularies evolved, they influenced one another, producing what came to be known as the "Verrocchian" style. This

Bertoldo di Giovanni
Medal with the Oath of the Pazzi and a Portrait of Giuliano de' Medici
1478
Bargello National Museum, Florence

explains why it is sometimes difficult to distinguish whose hands were at work in certain paintings.

Nevertheless, these young artists were all extremely gifted, and each had his own style and personality. Leonardo is described as personable, vigorous, intelligent, and generous, but also eccentric and unstable. It was said that Leonardo was a somewhat wild fellow, whose frenzy to learn was probably what led him to abandon so many projects half-begun, at least according to Vasari: "It is clear that Leonardo, through his comprehension of art, began many things and never finished one of them, since it seemed to him that the hand was not able to attain to the perfection of art in carrying out the things which he imagined; for the reason that he conceived in idea difficulties so subtle and so marvellous, that they could never be expressed by the hands, be they ever so excellent. And so many were his caprices, that, philosophizing of natural things, he set himself to seek out the properties of herbs, going on even to observe the motions of the heavens . . ." (pp. 627–628). His manner of dressing also was unconventional: his habit of wearing a short doublet and narrow breeches of blue or carmine velvet and silver brocade—quite different from the more usual long robes in sober colors—marked him as a unique personality.

By 1472 Leonardo was already enrolled as a member of the guild of Florentine painters, the Guild of Saint Luke (*Scuola di San Luca*), and therefore permitted to accept commissions in his own name, but two documents of 1476 attest to his continued presence in Verrocchio's workshop. Although Leonardo was already an independent artist, he continued to meet ever more demanding requests to collaborate on projects with his master for at least another four years. There was no shortage of occasions for learning new things, given the varied commissions the workshop received. A project that particularly interested the young man was the commission to make the great copper sphere to be set on the tip of the lantern of the dome of Santa Maria del Fiore, the cathedral of Florence. Verrocchio had been given the task of completing the cupola after the death of its designer, Filippo Brunelleschi, and since 1468 had been grappling with problems of casting and welding, and issues involving the design of the

Filippo Brunelleschi
The Dome of Florence Cathedral
1420–1436

11

scaffolding needed to support it. For Leonardo, this was an opportunity to come to grips with statistical and structural questions and inevitably led him to a close study of Brunelleschi's technical notes; he was fascinated by these and made numerous drawings of them.

When Verrocchio worked as a sculptor, it was his habit to make terra-cotta maquettes whose robes were made of pieces of cloth soaked in liquid clay. Some scholars point to this as the source of the technique of chiaroscuro sketching in brush on linen used by his students, especially in studies of drapery. Brush drawings of draperies were a test given by the head of the workshop to those who wished to become his apprentices. In more than one case—a drawing attributed to Lorenzo di Credi or a drapery study by Leonardo—the students showed a notable mastery of the brush in rendering the chiaroscuro effects of light and shadow in drapery folds through the use of white and black. This leads some scholars to claim that Leonardo is the author of *Madonna and Child with a Pomegranate (The Dreyfus Madonna)* (National Gallery of Art, Washington, D.C.), dated around 1469, the year Verrocchio went to the Veneto, possibly accompanied by Leonardo. That would explain the numerous similarities between this work and paintings by the Venetian artist Giovanni Bellini, seen in the color range used in the work, while the distinctive treatment of the draperies, articulated in artful folds in the foreground, seems to recall Leonardo's drawings on linen, mentioned above.

If so, then this is one of the very first works by Leonardo who, not yet twenty years old, was experimenting with the very human theme of the relationship between the Madonna and Child, to which he returned in several later works. Figures, architecture, and background do not seem entirely integrated yet, but that doesn't at all diminish the refined delicacy of the flesh tones or the sweetness of the whole composition. There is no other work like this in the oeuvre of Verrocchio or those of his other students. Since the painting has not been connected with any specific commission, we may speculate that this was a sort of "essay" assigned by the master to a new apprentice to measure his level of skill. Many of its details recur in subsequent works by Leonardo, but what most surprises is the innate precision of touch that delineates the details, such as the left hand of the Madonna or the gem

Above:
Giovanni Bellini
Madonna of the Little Trees
1487
Accademia, Venice

Opposite, with detail on the following pages:
Attributed to
Leonardo da Vinci
The Madonna and Child with a Pomegranate (The Dreyfus Madonna)
1469
Oil on panel, 6.18 x 5.04 inches (15.7 x 12.8 cm)
National Gallery of Art, Washington, D.C.

she wears at her throat, handled with an extremely delicate naturalism. In the same way, the color combinations anticipate those typical of the artist. Although the evanescent effects of Leonardo's famous *sfumato* shading are not yet visible here, other "Leonardesque" traits may be seen, such as the face of the Virgin, which is painted in successive layers of thin glazes, quite different from the decisive strokes of white used to define the draperies. On the other hand, the inserted passages of landscape, with mountains visible behind the figures, seem to have been added later. This was a common way of working in Verrocchio's workshop; such sections might be added or reworked in a painting by several hands.

Other works are true collaborations between the master and his students—for example, a work recently attributed to Verrocchio, the *Madonna and Child with Angels* (National Gallery, London), in which the hand of Leonardo may perhaps be detected in the handling of the lily held by the angel on the left and the rocky peak in the background landscape on the viewer's right. In fact, the first Leonardesque element has an almost exact counterpart in a signed drawing now in the Windsor Castle collection, which has the classic pinholes used for transferring a drawing to a painting. As for the rocky cliff, the scholars contend that it too was probably added later, over the background of hills, to enliven a landscape that was otherwise not naturalistic enough. This can be confirmed if we compare it with a landscape drawing of the valley of the Arno River that is Leonardo's first signed and dated work, dated August 5, 1473. The similarity of the tip of the rocky outcrop to that in the background of the painting is inescapable. The association permits us to place this collaboration of Leonardo and Verrocchio chronologically between the end of the 1460s and 1473. It is likely, therefore, that the master valued the work of this apprentice, who had by now achieved particular skill in the naturalistic rendering of plants and geological forms. His talent for such elements continued to be fed by a personal interest in direct observation and the study of nature.

Most scholars consider that Leonardo had a hand in another work attributed to Verrocchio, *Tobias and the Angel* (National Gallery, London). The little dog at the angel's feet was added at a second stage of painting, probably by Leonardo. The animal bears a close resemblance to a drawing by Leonardo in the Windsor collection, of later date than the painting. The similarity of that animal (a dragon) to the curly-haired dog in Verrocchio's work is unmistakable. It seems, therefore, that in more than one instance the student, young as he was, was free to contribute to the works of the master, and some discern his direct contribution even in some of Verrocchio's sculptures, such as *Lady with a Bunch of Flowers* (Bargello National Museum, Florence) or the *Doubting Thomas* group for the Church of the Orsanmichele.

Andrea del Verrocchio
and Leonardo da Vinci
**The Madonna and Child
with Angels**
ca. 1470
Tempera on panel,
37.8 x 27.17 inches
(96 x 69 cm)
National Gallery, London

The moment had arrived for Leonardo to execute his first solo work. As he was still a member of the workshop, this entailed trying his hand at a project arranged by his master. The attribution of *The Madonna of the Carnation*, completed between 1473 and 1478 (Alte Pinakothek, Munich), has been the subject of much debate. In this work, the graphic line typical of Verrocchio's style has been replaced by a new use of light for modeling volumes and a sculptural rendering of the figures. It resembles the *Dreyfus Madonna* in many respects, from the relationship between Mother and Child, to the opening out of the background landscape to the movement of the folds of cloth in the foreground—an element that turns up again in Leonardo's famous *Annunciation* in the Uffizi. Many scholars consider this painting a kind of general survey of his figurative universe: the naturalistic rendering of the draperies, which continues to appear in his subsequent works; the vision of the landscape, which already seems to be filtered through that *aria grossa* (thickened air), later described by Leonardo in his *Treatise on Painting*; the hairstyle of the Virgin, which anticipates the hair treatment in the *Leda* some thirty years later; not to mention a great capacity to use gestures to represent the internal tension that animates them. Powerfully evident, above all, is the artist's experimentation with a translucent surface to give mobility to light. In this he took advantage of the potential of oil paint, a medium that had only recently been introduced in Florence.

Between 1474 and 1476 he executed the *Portrait of Ginevra de' Benci* (National Gallery of Art, Washington, D.C.). Ginevra was a Florentine lady

Above:
Leonardo da Vinci
Study of a Dragon
ca. 1485–1489
Charcoal on paper
7.48 x 10.63 inches
(19 x 27 cm)
Royal Collection, Windsor

Opposite:
Andrea del Verrocchio and
Leonardo da Vinci
Tobias and the Angel
ca. 1478–1482
Tempera on panel
33.07 x 25.98 inches
(84 x 66 cm)
National Gallery, London

whose name is alluded to, according to the scholars, in the intertwined branches of palm, laurel, and juniper (*ginepro*) on the reverse of the panel. This symbolic meaning is made explicit in a painted scroll that wraps around the three plants, uniting them, and on which appears the motto VIRTUTEM FORMA DECORAT (BEAUTY DECORATES VIRTUE), referring to the gifts of the young lady in the portrait. The obverse bears the image of a woman scarcely past adolescence, probably executed on the occasion of her marriage, which took place in 1475. Leonardo here shows his "touch," using his fingertips to blur the surface of the painting around the eyes to make the skin seem alive and real. The stillness of the figure is countered by an imperceptible little puff of air that seems to set the plants and waters of the background fluttering.

It is an established fact that the artist knew the Benci family, for it was in the house of Amerigo, Ginevra's father, that Leonardo created the sketch for *The Adoration of the Magi*, on the eve of his departure for Milan. Nevertheless, there is also another hypothesis regarding the commission for this

portrait. Some argue that it was executed by Leonardo at the request of Bernardo Bembo, with whom he had an intellectual friendship in his youth. The landscape recalls that of the *Dreyfus Madonna*, although here the figure is set against a new, atmospheric vision of space. The student is poised to surpass his master—or so we are led to think, listening once more to the words of Vasari. Here he describes the collaboration between Verrocchio and Leonardo on the recently completed *Baptism of Christ*: "With Andrea del Verrocchio, who was making a panel-picture of S. John baptizing Christ, when Leonardo painted an angel who was holding some garments; and although he was but a lad, Leonardo executed it in such a manner that his angel was much better than the figures of Andrea; which was the reason that Andrea would never again touch colour, in disdain that a child should know more than he" (p. 628).

Although this anecdote is to be taken with a grain of salt, given that the two continued to work together thereafter, Vasari's comment conveys the degree of skill achieved by Leonardo by about 1478. Executed between 1475 and 1478 and intended for the Florentine Church of San Salvi, *The Baptism of Christ* is the fruit of a collaboration between the master and more than one of his

Above:
Andrea del Verrocchio
Lady with a Bunch of Flowers
ca. 1475–1480
Bargello National Museum, Florence

Opposite:
Leonardo da Vinci
The Madonna of the Carnation
1473–1478
Oil on canvas, 24.41 x 18.7 inches (62 x 47.5 cm)
Alte Pinakothek, Munich

students, among whom we may easily discern the hand of Leonardo in the figure of the angel looking over one shoulder, and the landscape at left.

The relationship of confidence and esteem that by now tied Verrocchio to Leonardo is confirmed—contradicting the words of Vasari—in the master's request that he and Lorenzo di Credi complete an important altarpiece for the Cathedral of Pistoia. Verrocchio, busy completing the great bronze equestrian *Colleoni Monument* in Venice, was often absent from Florence and did not hesitate to leave to his students the completion of a work he had already substantially carried forward. This is the *Madonna di Piazza*, begun around 1478 and worked on until about 1485. Leonardo painted part of the predella, a scene of *The Annunciation* (Musée du Louvre, Paris). Although the attribution to him is debated, the relationship between figures and setting seems Leonardesque, especially when compared with another *Annunciation*, unanimously attributed to him, today in the collection of the Uffizi Gallery. This latter work is sometimes dated to 1478 because of its close affinities with the earlier one, but it is likely that Leonardo had already worked on it for some years when he painted the Pistoia panel, beginning between 1472 and 1475.

A note in Leonardo's hand from 1478 refers to having started to work on two Madonna paintings, and a document of that same year records a commission he received for an altarpiece intended for the Chapel of San Bernardo in the Palazzo Vecchio, Florence's city hall. This was his first official commission, which he abandoned soon after. That was the year in which Leonardo left the workshop of Verrocchio and became an independent artist; at that time, at nearly thirty years of age, he also left his father's house and took his own lodging.

Florence at this time was at the acme of its splendor, thanks to the activities over several decades of the Medici family, culminating in the government of Lorenzo (1449–1492), and the political stability he established. Lorenzo, known as *il Magnifico*, or the Magnificent, was the son of Lucrezia Tornabuoni and Piero de' Medici and grandson of Cosimo il Vecchio (Cosimo the Old). He is celebrated as one of the great rulers of the Renaissance, hailed by the statesman Francesco Guicciardini as "the needle on the scales of Italian politics." Lorenzo was truly a brilliant leader and politician who repeatedly acted as intermediary between opposing forces and interests, and thus avoided conflicts and civil instability. He became head of the Tuscan capital in 1469 and promptly turned his attention to the internal ordering of the state; he soon succeeded in suppressing rivalries and resolving strife among the powerful families. He strictly limited democratic liberties without alienating the populace, reorganized civil statutes, and modified legal structures so as to consolidate his personal power. He also was able to establish good relations with other city-states through wise

Leonardo da Vinci
The Madonna of the Carnation (detail)

Left:
Leonardo da Vinci
**Portrait of
Ginevra
de' Benci**
1474–1476
Oil on panel, 15.28 x 14.45
inches (38.8 x 36.7 cm)
National Gallery of Art,
Washington, D.C.

Above:
Reverse of the panel

THE BAPTISM OF CHRIST

Verrocchio began this work, creating the general composition and painting part of Christ and the Baptist; it was then completed by some of his students. Characteristic of the master is the sculptural plasticity of the two central figures: His work as a sculptor led him to pay particular attention to anatomy and form through the clever use of chiaroscuro. Less expert hands may be discerned in the execution of God the Father at the top, the dove of the Holy Spirit, the palm at the left, and the landscape at the far right, although the identity of the artist who painted these elements is unknown. Most likely Verrocchio assigned his workshop students to complete the painting. It is thus by many hands, in particular two young and talented artists: Botticelli, who is responsible for the face of the angel seen in three-quarter view, and Leonardo. Some scholars claim that the painting was begun by another minor master, later turned over to Francesco Botticini, and then completed by the two great young Florentine masters. But in any case, all agree that Leonardo had a hand in it, as Vasari claimed, whereas the participation of Botticelli has been proposed purely on the basis of stylistic analysis, and is not supported by any documents of the period.

Francesco Albertini, writing in his *Memoir* in 1510, mentioned the presence at the Monastery of San Salvi of "an angel by Leonardo da Vinci." The painting then passed to the Vallombrosan Cloister of Santa Verdiana, where it was rediscovered in the nineteenth century by a commission established to inventory artworks and scientific objects housed in convents. Thus in 1810 it was brought to the Academy of Fine Arts in Florence and in 1914 was transferred to the Uffizi Gallery.

Opinion is unanimous that Leonardo contributed the figure of the angel at left, looking over one shoulder, and the glimpse of landscape beyond, both of which are characterized by that delicacy of touch typical of the Tuscan painter. Some scholars believe that, although several hands were at work in the painting, Verrocchio asked Leonardo to go over the whole and finish the composition, to give it some uniformity—an effect that he obtained by introducing the leftmost angel, who provides a diagonal that converges on the figure of Christ. Aside from this, what stands out about this figure is the naturalism of the profile, modeled with soft tones of shadow, and the curling hair, caressed with a gentle glowing light. A preparatory study for the

Right, with detail opposite:
Andrea del Verrocchio and Leonardo da Vinci
The Baptism of Christ
ca. 1475–1478
Uffizi Gallery, Florence

angel's head, now in Turin, shows a complex use of light and shadow that is transmuted in the painting into a physical and psychological elegance. The delicacy of the angel's face becomes the visual means by which interior feeling is expressed. With this figure Leonardo demonstrated his absolute command of the anatomy of the human figure and its placement in space, which was no longer based on the measurable, mathematical approach found in the art of the early 1400s.

The glimpse of landscape beyond the palm tree is another such demonstration of skill: There, in contrast to the rigidity of the tree, an expansive nature waits to be discovered, an open air that dissolves in the distance—a prelude to one of Leonardo's greatest innovations, his *sfumato*, or smokelike shading. This term is often cited to encapsulate Leonardo's pictorial mastery; it describes the progressive erasure of outlines, so that the edges of forms are eventually rendered completely invisible, as they appear in nature. In his *Treatise on Painting*, Leonardo wrote that in a painting the silhouettes must be blurred bit by bit so that the images recede into the background, because it is thus that they appear in reality. In consequence, everything in his works appears as if seen through a thin veil, an atmosphere that wraps the forms, enhancing the illusion that they exist in three-dimensional space.

It is likely that Leonardo also retouched the hair of the other angel and added glazing to the body of Christ to give greater realism to its anatomy without removing its softness.

use of his considerable diplomatic skills. He thus
became a key figure of the second half of the
fifteenth century.

Lorenzo had great cultural acumen and taste
and was the quintessential Renaissance patron. He
gave considerable impetus to the development of arts
and letters in Florence and was himself a scholar
and poet. He founded the Platonic Academy at his
villa at Careggi, where he gathered philosophers and
writers, most notably Marsilio Ficino and Pico della
Mirandola, to study and disseminate neoplatonic
ideas. Surrounded by men of letters, Lorenzo
supported the translation and study of classical texts
and critical commentary on them. He also cultivated
an interest in classical antiquity, adding to a
collection of ancient sculptures and precious objects
begun by Cosimo il Vecchio and later expanded by
Piero de' Medici. The collection of Lorenzo the
Magnificent was displayed in his palace in Via Larga
in Florence (today Via Cavour) and in the Garden of San Marco. This was a
kind of open-air storeroom for antique marbles and sculptures. Although there is
disagreement about the exact location and purpose of the garden, it is known that
Lorenzo invited young artists to study there and to examine his collections with
the intention of training them in the "perfection of art." Vasari handed down the
myth of an actual "school" held within the garden, and recorded the artists who
visited it. In 1488 Bertoldo di Giovanni, a student of Donatello and future teacher
of Michelangelo, was put in charge of it. Indeed, Vasari cited Michelangelo as
having frequented the garden, together with Giovan Francesco Rustici, Pietro
Torrigiano, Francesco Granacci, Lorenzo di Credi, and Andrea Sansovino. Thus
the Medici court of Lorenzo was soon filled with thinkers and artists. It is not by
chance, then, that (according to the so-called Anonimo Gaddiano, the unknown
Florentine chronicler who wrote several biographies of sculptors and painters in
1540) Leonardo "stayed as a young man with Lorenzo the Magnificent de'
Medici, who provided for him and gave him work in the garden in Piazza San
Marco in Florence." Probably he entered the Medicean garden soon after 1480,
and no doubt his interactions there with the official art world helped him to
increase his skills. Leonardo was by now fully formed, and the cultural world
that welcomed him was at the center of Italy and indeed of Europe. Since the
early 1400s Florence had led a revolution in art, beginning in the 1300s with
Giotto. The new pictorial language of the fifteenth century proposed a radical

Leonardo da Vinci
The Annunciation
ca. 1478–1485
Tempera and oil on panel
6.3 x 23.62 inches
(16 x 60 cm)
Musée du Louvre, Paris

transformation in the representation of the human figure, of space, and of the proportional relationships between figures and architecture. On the basis of the rediscovery of classical antiquity and of the value of nature, the artists of the Renaissance constructed a measurable space within which human figures were set realistically, thanks to the technique of one-point perspective developed by Brunelleschi as a scientific method for regulating spatial relationships. In Leonardo's time, the last generation of the Florentine 1400s boasted not only mature masters such as Verrocchio but also the great new names of Sandro Botticelli, Filippino Lippi (both active in the equally celebrated workshop of the Pollaiolo brothers), Piero di Cosimo, and Domenico Ghirlandaio—not to mention foreign artists whose works were brought to Florence by wealthy patrons. Indeed, the picture of fifteenth-century Florence would not be complete without those Flemish artists who, with their own specific stylistic language, contributed to the great revolution then under way, although the artists themselves are not known to have visited Florence. Artists such as Hugo van der Goes, Jan van Eyck, and Hans Memling—masters of rendering reflections of light, of details, and of the substance and materiality of things—contributed to a lively reciprocal artistic exchange between Florence and the cities north of the Alps. The Florentine eye was opened upon space; that of the north was focused on particulars. All this flowed together into a rich array of stimuli for Leonardo, who took it all in and developed his own personal and inimitable responses to it.

Right, with details on
the following pages:
Leonardo da Vinci
The Annunciation
ca. 1472–1475
Tempera and oil on panel
38.58 x 85.43 inches
(98 x 217 cm)
Uffizi Gallery, Florence

THE ANNUNCIATION

This painting, today in the Uffizi, comes from the Church of San Bartolomeo in Monte Oliveto, near Florence. Scholarship is nearly unanimous in considering it a work by Leonardo. The few doubts as to its authorship have to do with Leonardo's extreme youth at the time when it was painted, or with the fact that he apparently completed a work that had been begun by someone else. Some scholars suggest that the picture was born of collective ideas and contributions in the workshop of Verrocchio, and then passed into Leonardo's hands. The primary weakness of the work lies in the imperfect fusion of its parts into a unified whole, but this is mitigated by the extremely personal way in which the composition is constructed and the details defined.

The form of Mary's unusual bookstand apparently derives from the stone and bronze tomb of Giovanni and Piero de' Medici, designed by Verrocchio between 1470 and 1473 for the Church of San Lorenzo in Florence. This gives Leonardo's painting a date between 1472 and 1475, although some scholars place it around 1478, related to the Louvre *Annunciation*, a predella panel painted by the artist for the large Madonna di Piazza altarpiece in Pistoia. If so, then here Leonardo seems to be developing the idea of enlarging the same theme to the scale of the altarpiece, making a sort of "giant-size" predella, but another possibility is that he worked on it for several years until he amassed a compendium of all the teachings he had acquired in the workshop. In any case, if the painting shows a few errors, such as the overlong right arm of the Virgin with respect to the extreme closeness of the bookstand to the picture plane, nevertheless it is principally characterized by the cleverness with which the distant landscape relates to the foreground scene. The faces of the two figures display a grace that recalls something of Botticelli and yet is unique, thanks to the touch of Leonardo's fingers, which modeled the details of the features.

A close examination of the picture surface reveals numerous fingerprints of the artist, indicating how he executed the final modeling. The play of light and shadow is orchestrated with great mastery, beautifully exemplifying Vasari's description of Leonardo's chiaroscuro: "It is an extraordinary thing how that genius, in his desire to give the highest relief to the works that he made, went so far with dark shadows, in order to find the darkest possible grounds, that he sought for blacks which might make deeper shadows and be darker than other blacks, that by their means he might make his lights the brighter; and in the end this method turned out so dark that, no light remaining there, his picture had rather the character of things made to represent an effect of night, than the clear quality of daylight; which all came from seeking to give greater relief, and to achieve the final perfection of art" (p. 630).

Traditionally, *The Annunciation* was set in an interior; alternatively, the angel alone knelt in a garden or on a path, while the Virgin remained in her house, so that the idea of the visit by the angel could be depicted explicitly. Leonardo's great innovation was to set the entire scene outdoors, establishing a visual connection between Mary and the building behind her. Through its open door we spy a red bedcover, which conventionally refers to the house of the Virgin. The rhythm of the drapery folds guides the viewer's gaze toward the door and thence to the bed, so that a perfect coordination between figures and setting is established. Even the yellow drapery at Mary's waist, a symbol of her approaching pregnancy, is an innovation on the traditional iconography. Leonardo has derived this from Filippo Lippi; it replaces the usual image of God's impregnation of the Virgin in rays of gilded light borne by the dove of the Holy Spirit.

Opposite:
Leonardo da Vinci
The Annunciation
ca. 1472–1475 (detail)
Tempera and oil on panel
38.58 x 85.43 inches
(98 x 217 cm)
Uffizi Gallery, Florence

Above:
Giorgio Vasari
and assistants
**Lorenzo between
Philosophers
and Scholars**
1556–1558
Palazzo Vecchio, Florence

The Flemish capacity to render even the most minute details of reality perfectly tickled Leonardo's investigative spirit and encouraged his interest in the multiple aspects of reality. In his paintings this interest translated into a study of the naturalistic rendering of the tiniest variations in light and shadow, in landscape, in bodies in motion, and in the variety of human expressions. Furthermore, the Tuscan master was among the first to experiment with the technique of oil painting, which had been known in antiquity but was rediscovered and perfected in the latter half of the fifteenth century by Italian and Flemish artists. Legend has it that the Sicilian painter Antonello da Messina introduced oil painting to Italy through his contacts with Flemish culture at the Neapolitan court, where works and artists from the north were to be found. In reality, the matter appears to be rather more complex; recent studies have demonstrated that experiments with oil technique occurred more or less simultaneously in several Italian centers where Flemish artists were present.

For the rest, interest in this technique is understandable, for it offered numerous advantages. Compared with tempera, which is water-based and uses such substances as glue, gum, and egg emulsion as a medium for the pigments, oil paint uses an oily solvent, which dries slowly and is very flexible. This allows the painter to create translucent and brilliant surfaces, and to return to the painting again and again, layering transparent veils of color, or glazes, to achieve subtle refinements. This painting technique permitted Leonardo to achieve the subtleties of execution that characterize all his works.

The autograph note by Leonardo referred to earlier, in which he mentions working on two Madonnas, can be linked almost by consensus to a work of 1478–1481, his period of transition from student to independent artist. This is the *Benois Madonna* (State Hermitage Museum, St. Petersburg), which takes its name from the family that owned it until the early 1900s; it is also called *The Madonna of the Flower*. Several sketches on a sheet in the collection of the British Museum show Leonardo's first ideas for this composition, which is principally notable for the strong chiaroscuro that articulates the figures of the Virgin and the Child. Leonardo obtains this result through a calibrated contrast of two light sources, one coming from the upper left, the other from a window in the background wall. The extreme naturalism of the mother playing with her child is breathtaking; the artist confers on her gestures—and even more, on the general atmosphere of the scene—an unequaled tone of vivacity. Such perceptiveness is the fruit of direct observation of reality, enriched and strengthened by a knowledge of human anatomy in the Florentine tradition.

Above:
Hugo van der Goes
The Portinari Triptych
1476–1479
Uffizi Gallery, Florence

Opposite:
Leonardo da Vinci
The Benois Madonna (The Madonna of the Flower)
ca. 1478–1481,
Oil on panel,
transferred to canvas
18.9 x 12.2 inches
(48 x 31 cm)
State Hermitage Museum,
St. Petersburg

A clear example of this is the *Saint Jerome* (Pinacoteca Apostolica Vaticana, Rome), an unfinished painting for which we have no supporting documentation, but which Leonardo worked on around 1480. This picture reveals his interest in human anatomy and displays an absolute command of the space within which he has set the figure of the kneeling saint, restoring an almost real sense of three-dimensionality. Some scholars believe that Leonardo abandoned the work because he was dissatisfied with the excessive length of the left arm stretching forward, but it is precisely its incompleteness that affords us the opportunity to observe the artist's process at the sketch stage of a panel. The body of the saint has almost sculptural articulations, and the tension of his attitude is an efficient means of expressing the internal drama he is experiencing. He is captured in a moment of unfolding action: His knee not yet resting on the ground suggests that he is in the act of rising, or, on the contrary, just sinking down from a standing position. The figure of the lion, too, is presented so as to convey the greatest possible naturalism, liberating it from its purely symbolic function in relation to the saint. Overall, this composition confirms Leonardo's rejection of the fifteenth-century typology in which a group of figures and objects is organized symmetrically; instead, he privileges a new conception of space that is more atmospheric and less geometric. The work's formal and structural characteristics, as well as its date, link it to *The Adoration of the Magi*, commissioned from Leonardo in March 1481 by the monks of San Donato a Scopeto. That work also remained unfinished because the artist left Florence for Milan, but it nevertheless remains at the pinnacle of the study of those "motions of the mind" (*moti dell'animo*, in Leonardo's famous phrase) that were constantly at the center of his pictorial and human inquiry.

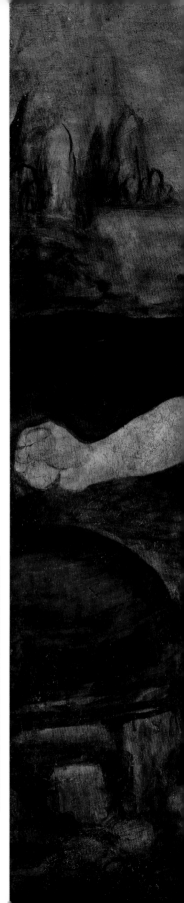

Leonardo da Vinci
Saint Jerome
ca. 1480, Oil on panel
40.55 x 29.53 inches
(103 x 75 cm)
Pinacoteca Apostolica
Vaticana, Rome

Pages 40–41
Leonardo da Vinci
**Perspective Study
for the Background of
The Adoration of the Magi**
ca. 1481, Pen, ink, traces of silverpoint,
and white lead on paper
6.42 x 11.42 inches
(16.3 x 29 cm)
Uffizi Gallery, Florence

THE ADORATION OF THE MAGI

At the acme of Leonardo's first Florentine period stands the unfinished *Adoration of the Magi*, the first work we can assign to him with some confidence, since it was a known commission. A contract survives for an altarpiece intended for the high altar of the Church of San Donato a Scopeto, dated March 1481 and requiring that the painting be completed within thirty months. When Leonardo departed for Milan in 1482 the unfinished picture was abandoned in the house of the Benci family, as Vasari recorded: "He began a picture of the Adoration of the Magi, containing many beautiful things, particularly the heads, which was in the house of Amerigo Benci, opposite the Loggia de' Peruzzi; and this, also, remained unfinished, like his other works" (p. 631). In 1496 Filippino Lippi painted the same theme for the monks, following Leonardo's conception of it in many respects.

Although Leonardo's work remains in a sketchy state, it summarizes his figurative aims until that moment: an unparalleled whirlwind of gestures, expressions, and interior emotions. Once again he recast tradition, setting the moment of the Epiphany out-of-doors rather than within a shed or hut, as was usual. It is placed off-center, to the right, and is scarcely visible because the center is wholly occupied by the figure of the Virgin with the Child on her arm. This central group, together with two of the Magi kneeling at left and right in the foreground, forms a triangle that constitutes the fulcrum from which the complex and dynamic articulation of the entire scene radiates. No one's pose is static, because the tension of the event infuses every element of the composition. Leonardo made many sketches and studies for this work in order to create this collection of convulsive poses, gestures, and emotional expressions, which translate into visual terms the shock produced by the Revelation.

Right, with detail on the following pages:
Leonardo da Vinci
The Adoration of the Magi
ca. 1481–1482
Oil on panel
96.85 x 96.46 inches
(246 x 245 cm)
Uffizi Gallery, Florence

Each figure is thought out in both its own internal dimension and the resulting external manifestation, and the incompleteness of the work, like the *Saint Jerome*, gives us some insight into how Leonardo worked. The artist constructed a play of volumes on a preparatory ground using dark brushwork, without laying other colors onto the support, so that the parts that thrust forward are illuminated and surrounded by zones of shadow done in crosshatched bister, a blue-black pigment. He created an extraordinary variety of psychological reactions to the event; astonishing, too, is the attention given to the construction of space, which recedes along a diagonal axis marked by two aligned trees. All is movement and vibration, thanks above all to the lively brushstrokes, which are left visible and to which the artist added touches of color obtained with minimal variations in tone. Some interpreters have identified the standing figure at far right as Leonardo's self-portrait, as if he wished to participate as stage director in the convulsive dynamism of the scene.

Below:
Leonardo da Vinci
Drawings of heads,
probably studies for
**The Adoration
of the Magi** 1478
Pen and ink on paper
Department of Prints
and Drawings,
Uffizi Gallery, Florence

Right:
Leonardo da Vinci
Studies for **The Adoration
of the Magi** ca. 1481
Metalpoint, pen,
and ink on canvas
Department of Drawings,
Musée du Louvre, Paris

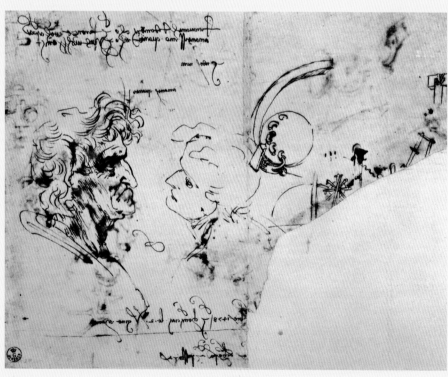

Chapter 2
In Milan at the Court of Ludovico il Moro

Equal in splendor to the Florence of Lorenzo the Magnificent, the duchy of Milan of Ludovico Sforza, called il Moro (1452–1508), was a vibrant cultural center in the Italian landscape that attracted numerous intellectuals and artists. This was due largely to the efforts of Ludovico himself. Son of Francesco Sforza, Ludovico succeeded his brother Galeazzo Maria as regent of the duchy in 1480. A refined patron as well as a capable diplomat, il Moro aimed to put Milan back on the world stage, first guaranteeing the political stability necessary for such ambitions. He garnered the support of the most influential ruling families, with whom he succeeded in establishing close ties, not least with the Holy Roman Emperor Maximilian Habsburg. Together with the pope and Lorenzo de' Medici himself, Ludovico forged a policy of "equilibrium" among the various Italian states and worked on the economic front to develop Milan's manufacturing capacity. He followed the example of Lorenzo the Magnificent in the attempt to lend his court an atmosphere of intellectual activity, surrounding himself with persons of note on the contemporary literary and artistic scene.

Following in the footsteps of other noble families, not only the Medici of Florence but also the Montefeltro of Urbino and the Este of Ferrara, the duke of Milan brought together a circle of erudite and artistic figures who helped to give the city a high profile in all areas of art and culture. Milan was singularly prominent in artistic production: Here the remnants of the old International Gothic style, which had been so widespread in previous decades in the cities of northern Italy, met the newest inventions of the Renaissance artists, who gravitated to the Sforza court from all points. So Ludovico's invitation to come to Milan in 1482, when Leonardo was thirty, was a unique opportunity for him to work in a context with many influences—perhaps lacking the cultural unity of Medici Florence, but undoubtedly rich in new stimuli for the Tuscan.

By now Leonardo was an experienced artist, having matured during his years in Verrocchio's workshop and as an independent artist. At the explicit request of Ludovico Sforza, Lorenzo the Magnificent sent him as a "cultural ambassador" from Florence to the Lombard capital, a role that indicates the esteem in which

49

Leonardo's talent was already held, as one of the greatest expressions of Florentine art.

Curiously, Leonardo also wrote a letter of self-presentation to Ludovico il Moro, in which he enumerated the breadth of his skills, indicating the various "services" that he could render to the duke of Milan, and only at the end mentioning his abilities in "painting and marble, bronze, and clay sculpture," and in the creation of "public and private buildings." Leonardo was a pioneer in the development of a new kind of court artist—versatile and universal; he emphasized his skills as a military engineer and man of science, capable of constructing war machines of "beautiful and useful form," bridges and military apparatus, and sophisticated devices minutely documented in his manuscripts. Well aware of the valuable opportunity offered him by Ludovico's invitation, Leonardo clearly expressed his desire to pursue his own simultaneous research in military and civil engineering, architecture, and physics while in Milan. Indeed, with passion and a scrupulous investigative method, during the years he stayed there, he explored the most varied problems in the fields of the natural sciences, one by one—studies in mechanics, optics, ballistics. His witty eclecticism and the dexterity with which he experimented in diverse disciplines were much admired by Ludovico, who availed himself of Leonardo's ingenuity even to design theater sets and decorations for temporary masques—for example, for the festivities for Ludovico's wedding to Beatrice d'Este in 1491. Thus Leonardo interspersed his work in science and anatomy with inventing mottos and emblems and creating clever games, toys, and costumes. Equally curious is the reason he was sent to Milan—at least, according to Vasari, who claimed that Leonardo was expert at

Above:
Nicola Cianfanelli
Leonardo Describes His Artistic and Mechanical Inventions to Ludovico Sforza
1842
The University of Florence, Tribune of Galileo

Opposite:
Leonardo da Vinci
Study for the Sforza Monument
1491–1493
Black charcoal on paper
10.95 x 7.24 inches
(27.8 x 18.4 cm)
Royal Library, Windsor

playing the lyre, and "was summoned to Milan in great repute to the Duke, who took much delight in the sound of the lyre, to the end that he might play it: and Leonardo took with him that instrument which he had made with his own hands . . . with which he surpassed all the musicians who had come together there to play. Besides this, he was the best improviser in verse of his day" (p. 631).

And it is once again Vasari who tells us of one of Leonardo's most ambitious projects for Ludovico, a bronze monument, "a horse in bronze, of a marvellous greatness, in order to place upon it, as a memorial, the image of the Duke," Francesco Sforza (p. 633). Indeed, Leonardo ended his famous letter to Ludovico with an offer to make an effigy on horseback of the founder of the house of Sforza, following a well-established artistic tradition. This task was to keep him occupied for the better part of the next fifteen years, yet he never completed the work. From the first sketches Leonardo created in 1485, it is clear that he intended to break with the tradition of the equestrian statue, using a compositional schema that was altogether new and unusual. He conceived of a rider seated on a rearing horse, under whose forehooves lay a supine figure. Notwithstanding the undoubted expressive power of the idea, Leonardo abandoned that version, which posed insurmountable technical difficulties, returning to the project at the beginning of the 1490s with a less daring version in which the horse was shown at a trot. He completed a terra-cotta model in 1493. This was, according to eyewitness records, a staggering colossus more than seven meters high, but the quantity of metal needed for the casting of a final bronze version never became available. In 1499 the troops of King Louis XII of France, who claimed sovereignty over the duchy of Milan, invaded the city and destroyed the work, which had been standing in the courtyard of the Castello Sforzesco, the great fortified castle in the center of Milan that was the seat of Ludovico's government. Today, only a few preparatory drawings survive.

But it was in his intensive activity as a painter during the Milan years that Leonardo achieved his greatest results. Delving deep into the study of nature and developing his own criteria for research, he accomplished marvels so resonant as to influence the entire future course of art. In his Milan projects he returned to an investigation of the complex relationship between figures and the landscape in which they were set, as he had done in his Florentine panels; but the masterpieces he produced for Ludovico constituted another step forward, beginning with a more mature and conscious approach to the study of nature, the result of reflections on painting he had developed in the environment of the court.

One example is the first work he produced in Milan beginning in April 1483, a commission from the Confraternity of the Immaculate Conception to paint a polyptych for the high altar of the Chapel of the Confraternity in the

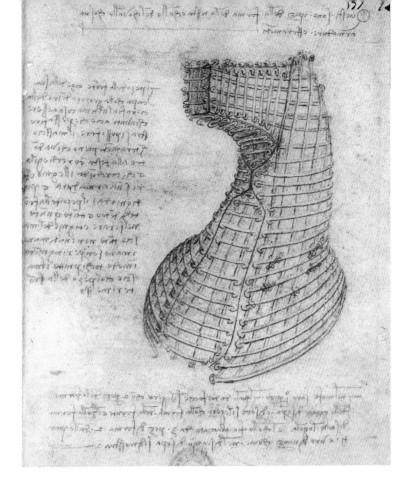

Convent of San Francesco Grande, which was unfortunately demolished in 1576. Leonardo was assisted in painting the panels by two of his students, the brothers Ambrogio and Evangelista de' Predis. According to the highly detailed contract with the Franciscans, the work was to consist of a composition with Mary and the Christ Child flanked by two prophets and angels. Freeing himself from the limitations imposed by the contract, Leonardo interpreted the theme in a liberal manner and produced a work that is as hotly debated as it is important to the history of art, and known as *The Virgin of the Rocks* (first version, Musée du Louvre, Paris).

In fact, a different version of *The Virgin of the Rocks* (second version, National Gallery, London) was eventually consigned to the confraternity in 1508, varying in certain important details from the first interpretation. Leonardo's reason for making these changes to the second version may be that the first, enigmatic version proved difficult to understand. It was sent by Ludovico as a gift to Maximilian Habsburg in 1493, on the occasion of his marriage to Bianca Maria Sforza; but the question of why there are two versions remains unresolved, although many plausible explanations have been proposed.

THE VIRGIN OF THE ROCKS (FIRST VERSION)

The Virgin of the Rocks was the first work Leonardo made during his stay in Milan. It was commissioned in 1483 by the Confraternity of the Immaculate Conception and was intended to occupy the center of an elaborate carved-wood altarpiece, the work of several collaborating artists. The frame was carved and sculpted by Giacomo del Maino between 1480 and 1482, while the brothers Ambrogio and Evangelista de' Predis, Leonardo's collaborators, completed the two side panels with music-making angels (National Gallery, London) and the tinting and gilding of the woodwork. Following the demolition of the Chapel of the Conception in 1576, the altarpiece was dismantled and probably modified and recomposed, together with all the chapel's decorations, in another location within the church. With the suppression of the convent and church in the eighteenth century, the wooden altarpiece was once more dismantled and was dispersed, so that it is now difficult to reconstruct its original appearance. Leonardo's panel was transferred to canvas in 1841, so that today no marks or fastenings on the original support survive to indicate the exact position of the parts of the polyptych. The contract between the artists and members of the confraternity called for a cluster of panels: a central panel representing an "Our Lady"—that is, the Virgin—surrounded by two prophets and angels and two side panels bearing four music-making angels on one side and four singing angels on the other. Because the overall structure of the work has been lost, it is not easy to evaluate the discrepancies between the description in the documents and the paintings that have come down to us. Some aspects of Leonardo's work are revealed, however, in a petition he and Ambrogio de' Predis sent to Ludovico il Moro after 1491 (when Ambrogio's brother Evangelista died), in which the two artists ask for an increase in the compensation due them for the work and request that a commission of inquiry be appointed to assess its value. It can therefore be deduced that at the beginning of the 1490s *The Virgin of the Rocks* had been completed—although presumably it was never delivered to the confraternity; instead, a second version was completed in 1508. That version is now in the National Gallery, London. Just why Leonardo produced a second *The Virgin of the Rocks* remains an open question. It seems likely that the commissioning patrons had strong objections to

Right:
Leonardo da Vinci
Study for the Face of the Angel of The Virgin of the Rocks
ca. 1483, Silverpoint and white lead on prepared paper,
7.13 x 6.26 inches (18.1 x 15.9 cm)
National Library, Turin

Opposite, with details on the following pages:
Leonardo da Vinci
The Virgin of the Rocks (first version)
ca. 1483–1492
Oil on panel transferred to canvas,
Musée du Louvre, Paris

certain ambiguities and difficulties of interpretation in the iconography of the Louvre painting. In depicting the legend of a meeting of the infant Saint John and the Christ Child in the desert, the artist chose to set the scene within an unusual rocky landscape, thick with vegetation, in a sort of cavern illuminated by light filtered through outcroppings in the cliffs. The figures, seated before the grotto, are organized in a precise pyramidal schema whose apex is the Virgin, firmly set between the others in a tight arrangement of gestures and gazes. The fact that Christ is not the central figure—and indeed is identified only by the blessing gesture of Mary's hand—the absence of halos, the preeminence of the figure of the young Saint John, the almost animal appearance of the angel who points to him (and whom some critics have likened to a harpy) all may explain the reluctance of the confraternity to accept delivery of the painting and their request for a revised version. Paradoxically, the painting that suffered so hostile a reception initially has been appreciated in succeeding centuries for its wealth of innovations; since the eighteenth century it has been one of the most celebrated and copied works in Leonardo's oeuvre.

Left:
Leonardo da Vinci
**Star of Bethlehem,
Wood Anemone and Sun
Spurge (Study for Leda)**
1505–1507
Royal Library, Windsor

Opposite:
Leonardo da Vinci
**Cliffs with Water Birds,
(Probably a Study for
The Virgin of the Rocks)**
ca. 1482–1485
Pen and ink on paper
8.66 x 6.22 inches
(22 x 15.8 cm)
Royal Library, Windsor

Another area of art that Leonardo helped to profoundly revitalize during his Milan years was portraiture. His portraits offered new, modern, and original approaches to representation, comprising skillful studies of physiognomy, a plastic sense of form, and ideas derived from Flemish painting. Leonardo built upon the work of the painter Antonello da Messina, who had abandoned the traditional profile portrait based on coins and medals in favor of a three-quarter view of the subject, set against a uniform dark ground—and not by chance, for Antonello himself apparently visited Milan in 1475.

Leonardo's portraits were the occasion for a further exploration of the relationship of figure to surrounding space. In them, as in the earlier *Ginevra de' Benci*, he drew upon the skills he had developed under Verrocchio, but made his figures even more "sculptural" and at the same time dynamic, expressing their solidity of form through ingenious tricks of light.

Thus, in the only male portrait he produced, *The Musician* (Pinacoteca Ambrosiana, Milan), most likely completed around 1485, he portrays a young man whose intense gaze is directed with utter concentration to the right, beyond the edge of the picture. A strong light illuminates his face, strengthening a potent, variable chiaroscuro that fragments across his cheekbones, his chin, and his nose in unexpected glints of light and sharp shadows. The touches of light and shadow in the thick hair spilling from his red beret, are more tenuous and vibrant. The part of his dress now painted black was, apparently, also originally red. We should pay special attention to the hand that holds a scroll near the bottom edge of the picture. This was discovered only when the work was conserved at the beginning of the twentieth century, thanks to which several layers of later overpainting were removed; but the technique in which the hand is executed is sufficiently different from the rest of the work to suggest that it was a later addition, possibly not by Leonardo.

As far as the identity of the sitter is concerned, many doubts remain: He has been variously identified as Franchino Gaffurio, music director of the Cathedral of Milan in 1484, and as Josqin des Prèz, a French composer also active in the cathedral at the time. Beyond the identification, the Ambrosiana *Musician* is striking for the strong magnetism of the figure and its solid structure. In this work Leonardo demonstrates a deep knowledge of the portraiture techniques of the Flemish masters and focuses on the close relationship between the psychology of the sitter and the action he is carrying out. He places his emphasis on the man's concentration, caught as he is in the moment of silence just before the music begins.

If *The Musician* is distinguished by a certain sense of suspension and meditation, the other portraits on which Leonardo worked during his Milanese years register a radical change of direction, a turning point in that exploration of

Leonardo da Vinci
Sketch for The Madonna of the Cat
ca. 1478
Pen and ink on paper
11.06 x 7.84 inches
(28.1 x 19.9 cm)
British Museum, London

the "motions of the mind" so dear to the artist. Paradigmatic in this sense is the portrait best known as *The Lady with an Ermine* (Czartoryski Collection, Cracow), which Leonardo probably began in 1488. In this work he gave form to all his reflections on the sense of volume of figures and the study of light— possibly somewhat weakened by the overpainting of a window that originally appeared behind the lady's left shoulder, an element revealed by x-rays taken of the panel. Even so, the rhythmic construction of the whole work gives it great originality, and its effect is in no way diminished by the somewhat perfunctory definition of some details, such as the left hand, or by what are probably several later additions to the hair and clothes.

Closely associated with *The Musician* and *The Lady* of Cracow in its similar spatial placement and the study of contrasts of light and shadow is the last of the portraits that Leonardo executed at the Sforza court, known to the general public by the title *La Belle Ferronière*, or *Portrait of a Lady* (Musée du Louvre, Paris). The name is based on an error that occurred during a cataloguing of works in the eighteenth century, when the painting was confused in an inventory with another portrait, of the "beautiful wife of an ironmonger," a lover of Francesco I. The features Leonardo was reproducing in this panel, datable to around 1495, were probably those of Lucrezia Crivelli, the lover of Ludovico Sforza, with whom the duke had a child in 1497. Several other identifications have also been proposed: that it is a portrait of Cecilia Gallerani (who is more likely identified with *The Lady with an Ermine*), or Isabella of Aragon, for whom Leonardo was to have painted a portrait, which we discuss later, and which was never completed. In *La Belle Ferronière* Leonardo once again approached stylistic solutions he had already tried in other Milanese portraits, beginning with the dense black background from which the lady emerges, in half-bust, revealed by a powerful light source. The spiral effect of the figure's pose is decidedly less vivid than in *The Lady with an Ermine*, although it is suggested by the tilt of the head to the right with respect to the direction the bust is facing, and by her elusive glance, past the viewer, which obliges us to move to the side in order to catch her eye. Leonardo further muffled the impression of dynamism in the figure by means of a false balustrade painted at the lower edge of the panel, which rebalances the composition, giving greater solidity and compactness to the whole. Finally, in this painting the artist seemed interested in pursuing his studies of the refraction of light on colored surfaces, which he carried out in tandem with other studies during his stay in Milan; in fact, the oval of the face appears to be little more than a pretext for rendering those pleasing passages of luminism that go from the rosy edge of the cheeks to the delicate pink and yellow tones in the areas more exposed to the light, sharply interrupted on the right side by the heavily repainted hair.

Leonardo da Vinci
The Musician
ca. 1485
Oil on panel
16.93 x 12.21 inches
(43 x 31 cm)
Pinacoteca Ambrosiana, Milan

Opposite, with details on
the following pages:
Leonardo da Vinci
**The Lady with
an Ermine**
ca. 1488–1490
Oil on panel
21.58 x 15.87 inches
(54.8 x 40.3 cm)
Czartoryski Collection,
Cracow

THE LADY WITH AN ERMINE

A letter sent in 1498 by Isabella d'Este, marchioness of Mantua, to Cecilia Gallerani, a Milanese noblewoman at the court of Ludovico il Moro, tells us that Leonardo executed for the latter "a portrait . . . from life" during his residency in the Lombard capital. The marchioness, a lady of great artistic cultivation, asks to be allowed to see the portrait, so that she may compare the work of the Tuscan master—whose fame had reached her—with other "handsome portraits" by Giovanni Bellini. This is the first documentation we have of one of Leonardo's most celebrated portraits. Scholars are nearly unanimous in considering this to be a portrait of Gallerani, lover of the duke of Milan and later wife of Count Bergamini. One clue supporting the proposed identification is the animal, whose name in Greek, *galî*, alludes to the young lady's surname as well as to her virtue. The painting was recorded in the Czartoryski Collection at the end of the eighteenth century; it was brought to Paris in 1842 and returned to Cracow around 1870, where today it hangs once more in the Czartoryski Collection, a public museum since 1876.

The Lady with an Ermine is paradigmatic in the development of Leonardo's painting. He abandoned the profile pose that was traditional for portraiture and instead presented the figure in a revolutionary rhythmic structure, an articulated rotary "movement" accentuated by the serpentine shape of the animal. The woman pivots, caught in an almost impromptu turn to the right; the little twist of the ermine in the same direction almost seems to imply that the painting is half of a diptych, a double portrait, and that it was originally paired with a second panel, perhaps the likeness of Ludovico himself. This supposition is, however, belied by the documents of the period, which refer to the portrait of Gallerani as an independent work. Leonardo merely made the painting more intriguing through the device of the lady's evasive gaze, which is cast beyond the edge of the frame. That this was a stand-alone work is also indicated by the exceptional precision with which the figure is articulated: Her emphatic rotation, in a hypothetical spiral that runs from the face down to the lower bust, is deftly balanced by the hand that holds the ermine, illuminated by an intense, strongly directed light. But the key attribute of *The Lady with an Ermine* is the highly studied correspondence between the figure's attitude and the emotion that shines in her eyes—that subtle "psychological" correlation between gestures and sentiments that the artist was at this time exploring in theoretical terms, and which was to find its greatest expression in the *Last Supper* fresco. *The Lady with an Ermine*, original and precious, is thus a pivotal work in Leonardo's artistic development.

Leonardo's masterwork par excellence in the Milan of Ludovico il Moro is without question *The Last Supper*, painted on a wall of the refectory of the Dominican Convent of Santa Maria delle Grazie. Ludovico commissioned Leonardo to paint a fresco of Christ's last supper—a theme reserved by artistic tradition for the walls of refectories—in 1494, when the duke decided that his family sepulcher would be located in the convent. Vasari described *The Last Supper* with enthusiasm as "a most beautiful and marvellous thing; . . . held by the Milanese in the greatest veneration, and also by strangers as well" for its extremely high quality and the scrupulous naturalism with which details are rendered—so much so, Vasari continued, that "even in the table-cloth the texture of the stuff is counterfeited in such a manner that linen itself could not seem more real" (p. 632). In this work Leonardo showed not only a consummate talent as a painter (in this work he used the technique of wall painting for the first time), but also absolute mastery as "stage director" of the whole scene, choosing to depict (and this is a fundamental point) the most dramatic moment of the last supper: that in which Christ announces to the Apostles that Judas will betray him. Sadly, the unfortunate history of the painting's poor state of conservation is all too well known; a mere twenty years after its creation it was already showing signs of deterioration caused by several factors, from the particular technique used by Leonardo to the dampness absorbed by the wall that bears the painting. Long years of restoration have only partly arrested the damage.

Although it does not succeed at the level of *The Last Supper*, another mural undertaken by Leonardo in 1497–1498 deserves mention, if only for the oddity of its subject matter: an intricate trelliswork arbor that covers an entire ceiling, demonstrating the particular attention to the natural world that was a constant in his studies. This work was a monumental mural painting covering the ceiling of a chamber in the northeast corner of the Castello Sforzesco. The room was commonly known as the *Sala delle Asse* (Chamber of the Wood Panels), a large room probably used for receptions.

A dubious restoration carried out in the early 1900s has distorted the original composition; some large areas where the original was lost were too freely repainted. Nevertheless, Leonardo created a powerful effect with the almost stage set–like composition of interlaced trees, which form a sort of architecture: Eighteen great tree trunks rise around the walls, and their branches intertwine on the shoulders and arches of the vault. The ceiling is covered with thick foliage, braided with gilded ropes; at the apex in the center the leafy branches part to reveal the heraldic coat of arms of the Sforza family in a burst of light. With this unusual work Leonardo clearly aimed to celebrate the magnificence of his patron, Ludovico. The duke's glory is also referred to

Right:
Leonardo da Vinci
**La Belle Ferronière
(Portrait of a Lady)**
ca. 1495
Oil on panel, 24.8 x 17.72 inches (63 x 45 cm)
Musée du Louvre, Paris

Following pages:
Leonardo da Vinci
The Last Supper
1494–1498
Tempera on plaster
181.1 x 346.46 inches (460 x 880 cm)
Refectory of Santa Maria delle Grazie, Milan

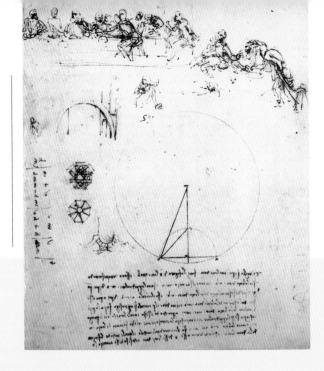

THE LAST SUPPER

Of the works created by Leonardo at the court of Ludovico Sforza, the greatest is indisputably *The Last Supper* in the Convent of Santa Maria delle Grazie, on which the artist worked for some four years. Commissioned by Ludovico in 1494, the painting was not yet done in 1497, as a letter written by the duke that year attests. In it he begged Leonardo to "finish the work he has begun in the Refectory of Santa Maria delle Grazie, so that he can turn his attention to the other wall of the refectory." The work must therefore have been completed in 1498, as is confirmed by a dedicatory letter to Ludovico il Moro with which the mathematician Luca Pacioli began his book *De divina proportione* (*On Divine Proportion*), a text in which he explored the geometry of the human body. Pacioli was an intellectual at the court of Milan and an old friend of Leonardo. In the introduction to his work, completed in February 1498, he mentioned the fresco in the Refectory of Santa Maria delle Grazie as a finished work.

Given the complexity of the scene that Leonardo chose to paint—the moment during the Last Supper when Christ announced his imminent betrayal by Judas, and the various reactions of the Apostles to the news—we may suppose that Leonardo made numerous studies and preparatory drawings of the composition, although only a few survive. Notwithstanding their meager number, these sketches show us that in the earliest stage of its development, the artist focused on rendering the range of the Disciples' gestures and expressions of distress. It is in precisely this that the genius of Leonardo's *Last Supper* resides. An expert in the human psyche, he populates his stage with an incredible variety of actions and attitudes, bringing to life an intensely dramatic composition in which the most varied feelings are expressed:

stupor, incredulity, dismay. Like an explosion spreading outward from the central figure of Christ, a wave of powerful anguish strikes and animates the Apostles, who are grouped in sets of three, linked by the overlaid and connected gestures of their hands and arms. Christ himself is perfectly inscribed within a triangle that acts as the fulcrum of the whole composition. The daring perspective, looking upward from below; the monumental scale of the figures; the multiple light sources—Leonardo uses each of these devices to augment the effect of astonishing intensity. The painting was done in tempera mixed with oil in two layers of plaster, which had a slower drying time than normal fresco, and thus permitted successive passages of retouching. Unfortunately, this working technique was one of the reasons *The Last Supper* deteriorated so quickly. Its worsening condition was already noted at the beginning of the sixteenth century. Successive heavy repaintings, water seeping through the supporting wall in several places, and the tragic bombing of 1943, during World War II, further aggravated the situation, long obscuring the fascination of one of the undisputed masterpieces of Italian art. The work's brilliance has been partly recovered in a recent, laborious conservation effort, conducted over the course of fifteen years with painstaking dedication and scientific rigor, which has brought stupefying details to light and revealed the marvelous luminosity of the colors.

Previous pages:
Leonardo da Vinci
Study for The Last Supper
ca. 1494–1495
Red chalk on paper
10.24 x 15.43 inches
(26 x 39.2 cm)
Accademia, Venice

Opposite:
Leonardo da Vinci
The Last Supper (detail)

Above:
Leonardo da Vinci
**Study for the Head of
Saint Bartholomew**
ca. 1495–1497
Red chalk on paper
Royal Library, Windsor

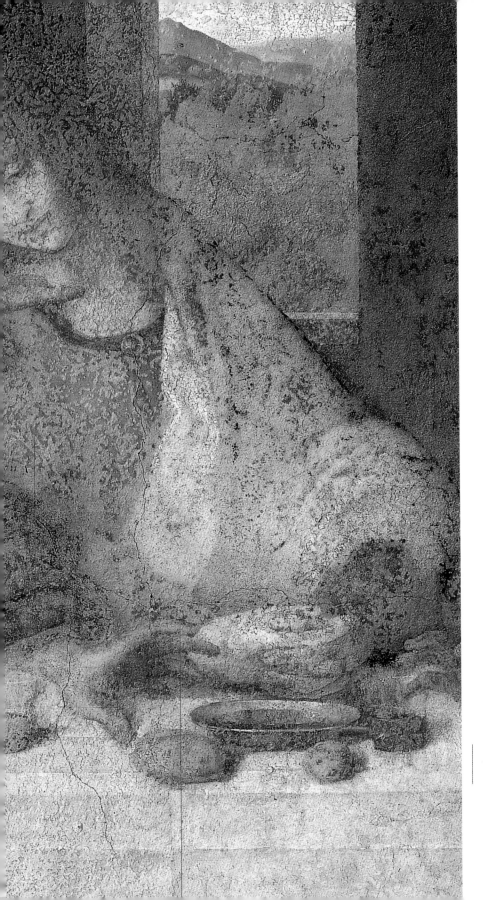

Leonardo da Vinci
The Last Supper
(detail)

79

Left:
Leonardo da Vinci
Study for the Head of James the Greater
ca. 1494–1498
Red chalk, pen,
and ink on paper
9.84 x 6.69 inches
(25 x 17 cm)
Royal Library, Windsor

Opposite:
Leonardo da Vinci
The Last Supper (detail)

Leonardo da Vinci
The Last Supper
(detail)

in the powerful tree trunks, which send their roots deep into equally robust rocky cliffs.

Scholars have often emphasized that the work can be read in symbolic terms: The trees are probably mulberries, a plant signifying prudence and wisdom, which may allude to the personality of Ludovico and to his skill in politics. In Italian, a mulberry tree is a *gelso-moro*; *moro*, meaning black or dark, also refers to Ludovico's nickname. In this work Leonardo once again reveals his extraordinary aptitude for depicting a bit of nature not merely as a purely formal decorative exercise but also to convey an allegorical and symbolic meaning.

Indeed, the dense composition represents the Vale of Tempe in Thessaly, that *locus amoenus*, with its luxuriant vegetation, that figures in so many classical texts. To create this scene, Leonardo availed himself of the assistance of his students—for he had by now formed a little band of artists, "followers" of his innovations in painting. This was the most immediate repercussion of his sojourn in Milan. It could not have been otherwise: A personality of eclectic talents, Leonardo attracted a close circle of collaborators who formed a virtual school in the Lombard capital, which essentially repeated the fundamental themes of Leonardo's own artistic path, at times hiding the results. Artists like Ambrogio de'Predis, with whom Leonardo had already collaborated on *The Virgin of the Rocks*, Giovanni Antonio Boltraffio, Marco d'Oggiono, and Bernardino Luini, Salai (Gian Giacomo Caprotti), are only a few of the students

Above:
Leonardo da Vinci
Decoration for the vaulted ceiling of the Sala delle Asse
1497–1498
Fresco
Castello Sforzesco, Milan

Opposite:
Coat of arms of the Sforza family in the vaulted ceiling of the Sala delle Asse
1497–1498
Fresco
Castello Sforzesco, Milan

Following pages:
Leonardo da Vinci
Rocks and Roots
Detail of the northeast wall of the Sala delle Asse
1497–1498
Fresco
Castello Sforzesco, Milan

with whom the artist established a long relationship of esteem and cooperation, as he himself noted; this collaboration spanned his years of intense work in Milan. Scholars have discerned the contributions of one or another of these students in Leonardo's works, above all in the marginal areas. Often their interventions are recognizable as a decidedly weaker version of the grace and rarefied atmosphere typical of Leonardo's art; not to mention those paintings long considered to be by the master's own hand, but later unanimously classified by scholars as "school of"—that is, done by one of Leonardo's followers.

Such a work is the *Madonna Litta* (State Hermitage Museum, St. Petersburg), which in the latter half of the nineteenth century was in the collection of the czar of Russia, Alexander II. The painting can be dated with confidence to Leonardo's Milan period; the studied, balanced relationship between the figures and the open windows of the background and their slightly melancholic elegance reveal its Leonardesque roots. Nonetheless, a certain hesitancy in the drawing and an altogether too accentuated chiaroscuro suggest that the *Madonna Litta* is either a work of collaboration between Leonardo and a member of his workshop or one that he left incomplete and that was finished by one of his students, almost certainly Boltraffio.

The artist's sojourn at the Sforza court ended in 1499, when events unexpectedly overtook him: The French king, Louis XII, having decided to reassert his sovereignty over the city of Milan, invaded the duchy with an army. Ludovico il Moro attempted to resist, but was badly beaten at the Battle of Novara in 1500 and condemned to exile in French territory. Leonardo was forced to leave the city where he had worked for more than fifteen years; in December 1499 he went to Mantua, to the court of the marchioness Isabella d'Este, one of his greatest admirers.

Isabella, a woman of immense culture, was a daughter of Eleanor of Aragon and sister of Ludovico's wife Beatrice, who had died in childbirth in 1497. She must have been familiar with Leonardo's extraordinary artistic skills; indeed, in 1498 she had asked that his celebrated portrait of Cecilia Gallerani, the so-called *Lady with an Ermine*, be sent to her so that she could admire his great talent for portraiture and his innovative results. Thus it

Above:
Leonardo da Vinci
Study with the Madonna Nursing and Profile Heads
ca. 1480
Pen and ink on paper
11.06 x 7.84 inches
(28.1 x 19.9 cm)
British Museum, London

Opposite, with detail on the following pages:
Leonardo da Vinci and a Collaborator
Madonna Litta
ca. 1490–1491
Oil and tempera on panel, transferred to canvas
16.54 x 12.99 inches
(42 x 33 cm)
State Hermitage Museum, St. Petersburg

came about that the marchioness commissioned Leonardo to paint two pictures for her, one of the Virgin and a second one with the figure of Christ at the age of twelve, as a letter in her hand dated May 27, 1501, attests. But the most important fact in the missive is her insistent request that Leonardo make "another sketch of our portrait." From this we infer that she already had one such portrait "sketch" in her possession—probably a cartoon (that is, a preparatory drawing for a panel). We may suppose that this drawing, made by Leonardo during his visit to Mantua, is the one now known as Portrait of Isabella d'Este (Musée du Louvre, Paris). It is a drawing on paper in black charcoal, red chalk, and yellow pastel, in which the artist has shown the marchioness in half-bust and, surprisingly, in profile.

Scholars have often noted that this drawing is pricked with the tiny holes used to transfer a drawing to a panel, and argued that this is evidence that it was indeed a preparatory drawing for a portrait painting, now perhaps lost. But the emphatic request of the marchioness and the dearth of information about this portrait suggest that Leonardo, occupied with numerous other projects, never painted it. Another fact to note is the rather loose manner in which the drawing is pierced for transfer: the holes follow the contours of the figure, correcting it in several places, suggesting how the artist intended to revise the final image. The rigid, dignified profile pose, enlivened only by the slight torsion of the bust, makes this image more traditional than the more experimental and dynamic portraits Leonardo completed in Milan— *The Lady with an Ermine*, for example. Perhaps this greater formality was by explicit request of Isabella, who may have wanted her portrait to be more majestic and solemn; but the attention given to the rendering of certain details, the way the hands are folded one over the other (reminiscent of the pose of the more famous *Mona Lisa* in the Louvre), and the grand scale of the figure, despite the small dimensions of the drawing, proclaim that this work is definitely by Leonardo.

It has also been suggested that Leonardo never finished the portrait of Isabella d'Este because he had undertaken so many other obligations at the time when he left Mantua in 1500. This time he went to Venice, having been

LVDOVICVS XII GAL:REX

hired by the leaders of the Republic on the lagoon. It was not his artistic skills that interested Venice, but his talents as a military engineer, as had been the case when he first went to the ducal court in Milan. With the same dedication and original thinking that he had shown as an artist in the preceding years, Leonardo picked up the threads of study that he had dropped in Milan: designing war machinery and showing that he was thoroughly familiar with the latest ideas of other military architects. At this time his manuscripts begin to fill once more with sketches of ideal fortifications and devices for defense, experiments in ballistics and plans for firearms, and observations on the most varied assault machinery, both land and naval. With this experience the great Tuscan genius added a final area of expertise to his rich portfolio of talents, already affirmed by the illustrious enterprises he had completed in the Milan years, before he returned once more to the city that had witnessed his earliest formation: Florence.

Above:
Cristofano dell'Altissimo
Portrait of Louis XII, King of France
before 1568
Uffizi Gallery, Florence

Opposite:
Leonardo da Vinci
Study for a Flying Machine
ca. 1478–1490
Pen and ink on paper
National Museum of Science and Industry, London

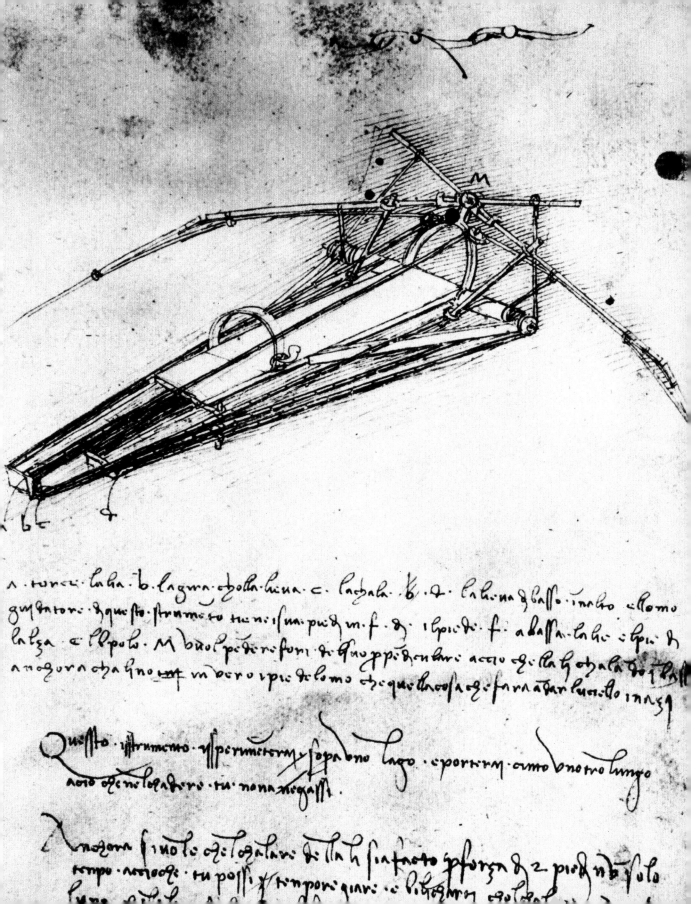

Chapter 3
Commissions at the Time of the Florentine Republic

When Leonardo returned to Florence in August 1500, he found the city profoundly changed in both political structure and general atmosphere. In the last decade of the fifteenth century, Florence passed through a great religious and political crisis caused by the confluence of a series of events, foremost among them the death of Lorenzo de' Medici in 1492. His government had maintained peace and harmony among its constituency; with his departure, internal dissension reemerged, as well as disputes with other Italian city-states. The inevitable consequence was the collapse of the fragile equilibrium that Lorenzo the Magnificent had been able to maintain. In 1494 Charles VIII of France came down into Italy to claim the Kingdom of Naples as heir of the Angevins. This sparked wars and battles between foreign and Italian armies. Inevitably, the echoes of these disturbances reached Florence, where a popular uprising overthrew the weak Piero, son of Lorenzo, and a republic was founded, led by the Dominican friar Girolamo Savonarola. Savonarola had been acclaimed in the city since 1482 as a preacher and interpreter of Holy Scripture in the Convent of San Marco; he had won the favor of Lorenzo and the humanists of his circle with ease, thanks to his high culture, reformist energy, and moral integrity.

Soon after taking power, Savonarola began to denounce the Roman corruption of the papal Curia with great ardor, inflaming the spirits of the masses; he explicitly opposed Pope Alexander VI (born Rodrigo Borgia) and demanded a reform of customs. Savonarola's polemic was aimed at both public and private morals, which in his opinion had become corrupt and dissolute. He called for a return to a pure and ascetic religious piety through which he could promote the wholesale reform of Florentine society, which he held up as an example for the world. Step by step, his ever more fervid sermons became tinged with anti-Medici and antihumanist accents—the neoplatonic doctrines that had been particularly admired in Lorenzo's cultural circle were now judged to be sinful, given their exaltation of humankind and of material beauty.

Art and culture could not help but be affected by such a climate; Florence was swept with a new culture of a pronounced devotional character, in sharp

Leonardo da Vinci
Head of a Young Girl (La Scapigliata) (detail)
ca. 1508
Oil on canvas
10.63 x 8.27 inches
(27 x 21 cm)
National Gallery, Parma

contrast to the humanistic culture of the preceding years, based on the cult of antiquity. Artists who had a taste for religious themes and compositional simplicity found a place in the new Florence, including Pietro Perugino; Lorenzo di Credi, who began to work exclusively on devotional works; and Filippino Lippi, who revived the medieval use of the gold ground in panel painting at the request of the Dominican friar.

Savonarola's republic was doomed to a short life, however; the situation came to a head in 1497, during a Carnival season that had been transformed into a festival of penitence—the infamous "Bonfire of the Vanities." A great bonfire was built in the main piazza of the city, and books, ornaments, luxury objects and rich clothing, mythological paintings, and pagan works were all thrown upon it. So extreme an act, together with a growing discontent on the part of the powerful bourgeoisie and the Medici party, not to mention the same crowds that until then had supported him, led to Savonarola's excommunication by the pope, who condemned him as rebel and heretic, "instrument of the Devil and the perdition of Florence." The dramatic ending of the story was his

Attributed to
Francesco Rosselli
**The Execution
of Savonarola**
ca. 1498
Museum of San Marco,
Florence

Sandro Botticelli
The Lamentation over the Dead Christ
1490–1492
Alte Pinakothek, Munich

execution. Savonarola was burned at the stake on May 23, 1498, in Piazza della Signoria, where today a plaque set in the pavement records his death.

Another artist whose career was closely linked with that of the preacher was Sandro Botticelli, whose shift in style toward greater austerity apparently reflects the religious crisis of those years. Some scholars, however, perceive a certain gloom in his works beginning earlier, in the early 1490s, and do not therefore believe that his stylistic choices were due to the influence of Savonarola, despite the marked change in the tone of his works. Apart from this critical debate, one fact is unarguable: In the last decade of the fifteenth century Botticelli began to depict Christian themes with a strikingly dramatic and passionate emotional quality that draws the viewer in. He turned his attention to the representation of religious subjects with a powerful expressivity, abandoning the scenes of pagan mythology for which he had been known, in response to a spiritual crisis that he personally experienced deeply. Works of this period include *The Lamentation over the Dead Christ* (Alte Pinakothek, Munich) of 1490–1492; one in the Poldi Pezzoli Museum in Milan, done a little later; and the *Mystic Nativity* (National Gallery, London), dated 1501, in which Botticelli seems to have abandoned the compositional conventions he developed in the course of the fifteenth century to return to more "archaic," or old-fashioned stylistic traits. The *Nativity*, for example, shows a marked lack of a strict perspectival structure, and proportional relationships among figures are based on their iconographic importance.

Botticelli knew, however, how to transform his own inner turmoil into a complete figurative language; in the case of another artist of the period, Bartolomeo Della Porta, personal crisis led to his temporarily abandoning painting altogether. Under the influence of Savonarola's condemning tongue, he took the habit of a Dominican monk, and only returned to painting around 1504, remaining committed to deeply devotional subjects. Not only were the older masters victims of the crisis, but the younger ones were, too, among them Michelangelo, who fled Florence after the Medici Palace was ransacked, and who viewed the event as the collapse of the ideal culture in which, until then, he had been raised.

The arc of Savonarola's rise and fall did not, however, lead to the end of the Florentine Republic. The government became oligarchic, with power concentrated in the hands of a *gonfaloniere*, a supreme magistrate. Thus was born the new bourgeois republic led by Pier Soderini, with the close assistance of Niccolò Machiavelli, a member of the Council. The Florentine Republic, which lasted until 1512, was modeled on the example of Venice, and was supported by the patrician ruling class and an environment favorable to the Medici. Closely associated with this new institutional structure was a renewed interest in public and private commissions for art, as an attempt to revive the cultural and artistic prestige that Florence had cultivated under the government of Lorenzo the Magnificent. But in contrast to Lorenzo's policy of sending his artists to work in other cities, the city now called its artists home, drawing them back with attractive offers of important projects with the aim of increasing the new government's credibility and authority through their works. It is in this context

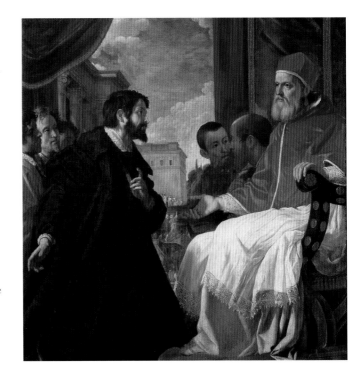

Anastasio Fontebuoni
Michelangelo Presents Himself to Julius II in Bologna 1620–1621
Casa Buonarroti, Florence

that Leonardo, by now a mature and fully formed artist, returned to Florence. Leaving Milan after the fall of Ludovico il Moro, he is known to have been in Florence by the end of August 1500, after having stopped for brief visits in Mantua and Venice en route to his hometown.

Vasari wrote, "He returned to Florence, where he found that the Servite Friars had entrusted to Filippino the painting of the panel for the high-altar of the Nunziata; whereupon Leonardo said that he would willingly have done such a work. Filippino, having heard this like the amiable fellow that he was, retired from the undertaking; and the friars, to the end that Leonardo might paint it, took him into their house meeting the expenses both of himself and of all his household; and thus he kept them in expectation for a long time, but never began anything. In the end, he made a cartoon containing a Madonna and a S. Anne, with a Christ, which not only caused all the craftsmen to marvel, but, when it was finished, men and women, young and old, continued for two days to flock for a sight of it to the room where it was, as if to a solemn festival, in order to gaze at the marvels of Leonardo" (p. 635). The veracity of this account is in many respects dubious; the historian referred to an *Annunciation* but then, describing the cartoon, mentioned the figures of Saint Anne, the Virgin, and young Saint John with the lamb. Actually, no preparatory drawing exists that depicts the young Saint John and the lamb together; nor is it possible to determine to what degree the work Vasari described corresponds to a commission for the high altar of the Church of the Santissima Annunziata. Often the details in Vasari's account do not perfectly match historical records, but in any case, his description confirms that Leonardo was with the Servite Friars at the beginning of the sixteenth century. And he did, in fact, take lodging in the Convent of the Santissima Annunziata when he first returned to Florence, although a bit later he went to live in the house of the mathematician Piero di Braccio Martelli, near the cathedral and the Medici Palace.

Setting aside the question of the relationship of the cartoon described by Vasari to the commission for the altarpiece, it is possible to detect in Vasari's narrative a point of contact with solid facts. Fra' Pietro da Novellara, vicar general of the Carmelite monastic order, wrote to Isabella d'Este on April 3, 1501, that Leonardo was painting "a Christ Child about one year old who is almost escaping from his mother's arms to grasp a lamb and who appears to be clutching it. His mother, rising from the lap of Saint Anne, grips the child to pull him away from the lamb. Saint Anne, also beginning to stand, seems to want to keep her daughter from separating the Child from the lamb. . . . And this sketch is unfinished." This description is from a letter written in response to a request from Isabella for a copy of the portrait of the vicar general drawn by Leonardo, who, however, seems to have been occupied with an entirely different piece of work. The description does not match that of Vasari, above all because Vasari mentioned a cartoon, whereas Novellara used the word *paints*, leading us to suppose that he was describing a panel painting not yet completed. Nevertheless, it is likely that the work displayed in the Church of the Santissima Annunziata, mentioned by Vasari, and the work described by Isabella's correspondent are one and the same, and that it relates to the Louvre's *Saint Anne, the Virgin, and Child with the Lamb*. Sticking to this hypothesis, we may suppose further that the cartoon cited by Vasari did once exist, but was later lost; therefore, we may presume that between 1501 and about 1510 Leonardo was working on the Louvre panel.

Even so, the question remains open, given the existence of the cartoon of *The Virgin and Child with Saint Anne and the Young Saint John the Baptist* (National Gallery, London), drawn in charcoal and white lead. Most scholars agree, however, that this work was begun by Leonardo in Milan during the last years of the fifteenth century. In this case, the drawing does not correspond to either Vasari's description or that of Novellara. Together with the drawing for a portrait of Isabella d'Este, the London cartoon is the only one that survives of many preparatory sketches for paintings that the artist no doubt created in the course of his career, above all when he was working on a project of a certain importance. Perhaps never translated into paint, the work was soon reprised almost literally by Bernardino Luini with the addition of a Saint Joseph, in his *Holy Family*, now in the Pinacoteca Ambrosiana in Milan.

Stylistic analysis, which notes an accentuated sculptural quality in the figures of Saint Anne and Mary, has led some scholars to date the cartoon in relation to a trip to Rome that Leonardo undertook around 1501, when he spent some time examining classical statuary, which affected his later style. Those who subscribe to this theory do not accept the dating of the cartoon to the last years of the 1400s, when the artist was still in Milan. One possibility is that when Leonardo returned from Rome to Florence he reworked an earlier sketch, developing the figures with a greater sculptural quality. This would suggest that the London cartoon reflects Leonardo's increased knowledge and study of classical art, attested to by numerous drawings he made during a visit to the ruins of the villa of the Roman emperor Hadrian at Tivoli. This would follow the development of

Opposite, with detail
on the following pages:
Leonardo da Vinci
**Cartoon for The Virgin
and Child with Saint
Anne and the Young
Saint John the Baptist**
ca. 1500
Charcoal and white
lead on paper
55.71 x 40.95 inches
(141.5 x 104 cm)
National Gallery, London

the version cited by Novellara, still unfinished in early April 1501.

In any case, the cartoon in question should be considered a work in itself, independent of the Louvre painting, since it is neither a first sketch nor a preparatory drawing for it. In the cartoon Leonardo conceived and executed a unified bloc of figures, but within this the emotions of each figure are clearly distinguished. As in all his works, the affective aspect predominates, constructed through the emotions of each figure, which even determine their poses and attitudes. The organization of the figures is not rigidly locked into a hierarchical, pyramidal structure, although Anne and Mary form the apex of the composition; since their heads are at the same height, they are engaged in an extremely intimate dialogue. Leonardo brought his full intelligence to bear on the delineation of these figures. Aware that each movement of the body must have another in compensation to maintain proper balance, he represented Mary in a state of both tension and stability. Although this is a cartoon, even here the scene is swathed in soft, atmospheric effects, created through alternations of light and shadow.

Leonardo's stay in Florence was interrupted by that brief trip to Rome, made at the invitation of Cesare Borgia, known as il Valentino, son of Pope Alexander VI. Whether or not this visit occurred in 1501, as those who consider the London cartoon to have been made after it believe, or in 1502, the fact remains that the invitation to Rome attests to the fame the artist by now enjoyed throughout the major Italian centers—and not only for his skills as a painter. In fact, the Pope brought him to Rome as his "Most Excellent and Most Beloved Private Architect and General Engineer," granting him a passport on August 18, 1502, to inspect all the forts and fortifications of the cities under Borgia rule. To that end, Leonardo left on a reconnaissance tour of Cesare's territories in central Italy, in the course of which he drew several important and exquisite maps. The artist's contact with Cesare Borgia may date as far back as 1499, when Cesare entered Milan with the army of Louis XII of France.

To stay in Rome meant to have the opportunity to deepen his knowledge of classical art, which Leonardo had first encountered in Lorenzo the Magnificent's Garden of San Marco in Florence. Now, however, his greater artistic maturity

Anonymous
**Portrait of
Cesare Borgia**
16th century
Palazzo Venezia, Rome

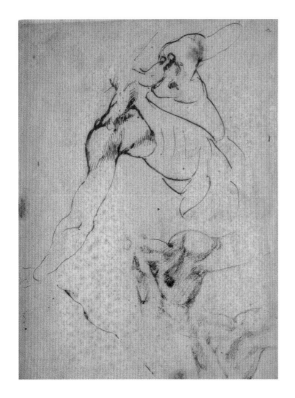

permitted him to carry out a more sophisticated analysis of it. A common view is that Leonardo's trip to Rome was the catalyst for a change in his pictorial style, toward more distinctly sculptural figures and a greater interest in the effects of chiaroscuro in draperies.

Leonardo returned to Florence in March 1503; according to Vasari, at this time the artist began the *Mona Lisa* and possibly the first drawings for *Leda*, but between July 24 and 26 he left once more, this time for Pisa to develop an engineering project (never carried out) to redirect the Arno River in order to deprive Pisa, Florence's rival, of its water source. His absence from Florence was, however, only temporary, for by now, as Vasari wrote, his reputation was well established: "By reason, then, of the excellence of the works of this most divine craftsman, his fame had so increased that all persons who took delight in art—nay, the whole city of Florence—desired that he should leave them some memorial, and it was being proposed everywhere that he should be commissioned to execute some great and notable work, whereby the commonwealth might be honoured and adorned by the great genius, grace and judgment that were seen in the works of Leonardo" (p. 636).

Thus in April 1503 Leonardo received a commission to execute one of two mural paintings for the Florentine government for the Great Council Chamber (*Sala del Gran Consiglio*), later known as the Hall of the Five Hundred (*Salone del Cinquecento*) in the Palazzo Vecchio. Soon, then, he returned to Florence to work exclusively on this new task, considered highly prestigious for the city. On October 18 he rejoined the Compagnia dei Pittori, the guild of painters, and on the 24th he received the keys to the Chamber of the Pope (*Sala del Papa*) in the Convent of Santa Maria Novella, placed at his disposal to use as a workshop and lodging while he worked on the preparatory cartoons for the mural. The city commission was for two great compositions depicting glorious moments in the history of Florence. The episode assigned to Leonardo was the Battle of Anghiari, which had taken place at Anghiari, near Arezzo, on June 29, 1440. The Florentines, led by Ludovico Scarampo and Piergiampaolo Orsini, together with allied papal forces, had defeated the army of the Duke of Milan, Francesco Maria Visconti, led by Niccolò and Francesco Piccinino. The other scene, whose commission was given to Michelangelo at almost the same time, was for the Battle of Cascina, in which the Florentines had won a victory over the Pisans in 1364. Such a commission denotes the high prestige of both artists, given that the Great Council Chamber was the meeting hall of the most important political organ of the Florentine government.

Construction of the room had been completed a little before 1500, and once the program of decoration was set, the Gonfaliere Pier Soderini had had no doubts about which artists to invite to execute it. It seems that Machiavelli was also familiar with the project. In October 1503 Leonardo entered Santa Maria Novella to start work on the cartoon, which did not begin until 1504. A work of such enormous dimensions and public importance constituted a tremendous undertaking for the artists and required constant attention by the whole Florentine government as well, so as to make the work go smoothly. One of the problems to be resolved was how to supply adequate lighting in so vast a room. A receipt for payment dated June 30, 1504, records the insertion of four windows into the western wall of the hall. This explains why Leonardo began to work relatively late, considering that the commission was from April of the previous year. Furthermore, at the beginning of 1504 he was already involved in another project: On January 25 he was asked to join a committee charged with deciding where to locate Michelangelo's *David* dating from 1501–1504 (Accademia, Florence); it was later set in front of the Palazzo Vecchio.

In any case, the artist was now involved in a massive endeavor; in May 1504 he signed a contract with the Florentine government that required him to present a finished cartoon for the mural by February 1505, and to begin the painting itself soon thereafter. In the meantime, Leonardo noted a sad bit of news he had recently received: "On the 9th of July 1504, Wednesday, at seven o'clock, died Ser Piero da Vinci, notary to the palace of the *podestà* [magistrature], my father: he was eighty years old, and left ten sons and two daughters."

Having made the cartoon, the artist turned to the work of transferring it to the wall. On February 28, 1505, the first of a series of payments was made for the construction of a movable scaffold in the hall of the Palazzo Vecchio, built by Giovanni di Andrea, father of Benvenuto Cellini. The purpose of the structure, designed by Leonardo himself, was to let the artist move along the wall while standing on it, so as to have greater mobility while painting. He planned to sketch out the work in its entirety, and then to work in detail on the whole surface, a project that contrasts with the more common method of fresco painting. Fresco usually requires rapid work, timed according to the drying time of the plaster spread on the area of wall being painted, so that the paint bonds completely into the wall structure through a chemical process. This means that the artist must paint while the plaster is wet, and therefore must work on one small area at a

Michelangelo
Study for The Battle of Cascina no. 73F
1504–1505
Casa Buonarroti, Florence

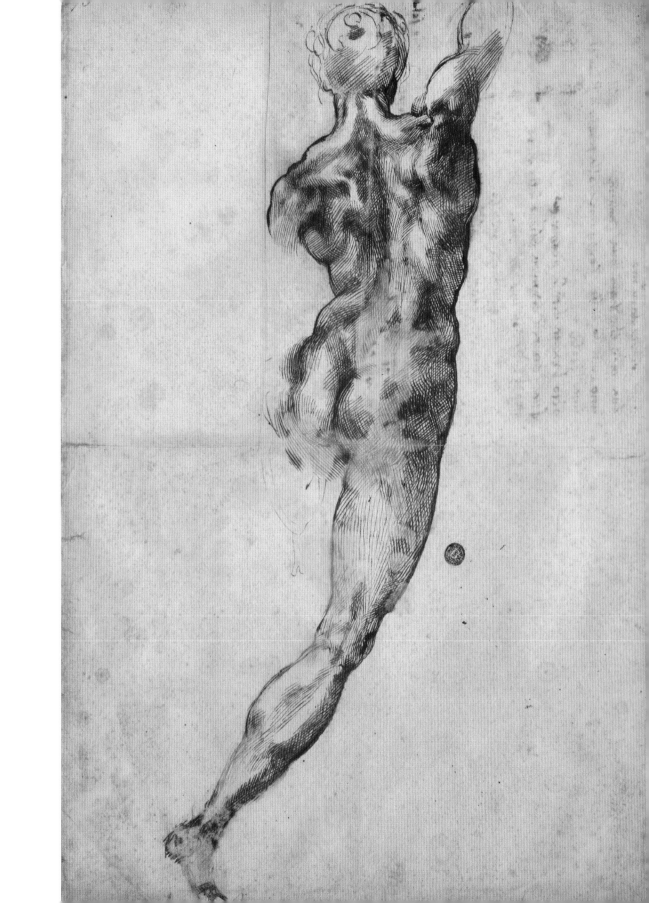

time. Probably it was the idea of working on the painting in separately finished sections in order to follow a slower, more pleasant rhythm that led Leonardo to decide to experiment with an alternative to traditional fresco technique.

Following some notes of Pliny on painting techniques, the artist prepared the stucco wall in a particular way, which he tested first on a panel. The result of that was positive and he was able to dry the compound rapidly with the use of heat. Work on the hall began on June 6, 1505, as Leonardo recorded in a note, in which he confessed that he thought he had witnessed a bad omen at the outset. Just as he was preparing to put the first brushstroke on the wall, a terrible thunderstorm broke out, which apparently damaged the cartoon. These are his words: "On June 6, 1505, Friday, at the stroke of 13 o'clock, I began to paint in the palace. Just as I was touching the brush to the wall the weather broke and the bell tolled calling men to cause [i.e., to court] and the cartoon tore and water poured down, and the water jar broke . . . and heavy rain poured down until nightfall and the day turned dark as night."

The fate of *The Battle of Anghiari* was indeed sealed: The anonymous Florentine chronicler who wrote at the end of the first half of the sixteenth century records that Leonardo was about to dry some finished areas of the painting with fire when the upper surface began to peel away and fell to the floor. Another bad omen? Perhaps for the artist, yes. The fact remains,

Bastiano da Sangallo
The Battle of Cascina
copy after Michelangelo
Leicester Collection, Norfolk

unfortunately, that the experimental impulse in Leonardo did not, in this case, result in the creation of the splendid image he had in mind. Shifting from panel to mural, the painting technique he had developed did not work well, since the fire lit in the chamber did not dry the paint quickly enough, so it ran. The companion painting that Michelangelo was preparing to paint suffered almost the same fate: it too was destined never to be admired by future generations. His picture got as far as the cartoon—a work that has provided whole generations of artists with an abundant sampler of male nude studies in a great variety of poses of muscular tension. As for the wall paintings themselves, no trace remains of either of these memorable efforts, of which the sculptor Benvenuto Cellini remarked that "as long as they survived they served as a school for all the world."

For his part, Leonardo managed to paint a small part of the episode, which must have remained visible for some time before it disappeared, for a number of extant copies offer evidence of what it looked like. The completed section depicted the battle of cavalrymen to capture the battle flag; it is known as *The Fight for the Standard* and was copied by numerous artists. There are some documentary records as well: Around 1510 Francesco Albertini mentioned it in his *Memoir*; in 1513 a scaffold was erected to repair what is referred to as the "painted wall"; in 1549 Anton Francesco Doni, writing to Alberto Lollio in Venice described things worth seeing in Florence, and invited him to visit the "great chamber to take a look at a group of horses and men . . . a battle-piece by Leonardo da Vinci that you will think miraculous." Although it is not possible to envision Leonardo's work in all its details, many proposals have been developed that attempt to reconstruct it. Scholars have examined the

Michelangelo
David
1501–1504
Marble
203.54 inches
(517 cm) (height)
Accademia, Florence

111

numerous surviving sketches that Leonardo made as he was working out the composition. Whereas the copies that have come down to us reproduce only *The Fight for the Standard*, Leonardo's drawings show other parts of the battle as well, probably intended for other areas of the immense scene; these give us some idea of what the complete work might have looked like. Most likely, the artist based the composition on written descriptions of the battle. This gave him the opportunity to display the horror of combat and the intensity of the emotions that accompany great physical effort, and also to ensure that the work would be legible by not introducing too many figures. This is a principle Leonardo emphasized in his so-called *Treatise on Painting* (a posthumous compilation of extracts on painting taken from his various manuscripts, and assembled around 1550). He wrote: "Pictorial narrative should not be burdened or rendered confusing by too many figures."

Beyond the various more or less persuasive hypotheses, it is uncertain just what was so remarkable about this painting before it was covered over by frescoes executed by Vasari between 1563 and 1572, when the chamber was turned into the Hall of the Five Hundred. But Vasari himself provided a vivid description: "Leonardo . . . designed a group of horsemen who were fighting for a standard, a work that was held to be very excellent and of great mastery, by reason of the marvelous ideas that he had in composing that battle; seeing that in it rage, fury and revenge are perceived as much in the men as in the horses, among which two with the fore-legs interlocked are fighting no less fiercely with their teeth than those who are riding them do in fighting for that

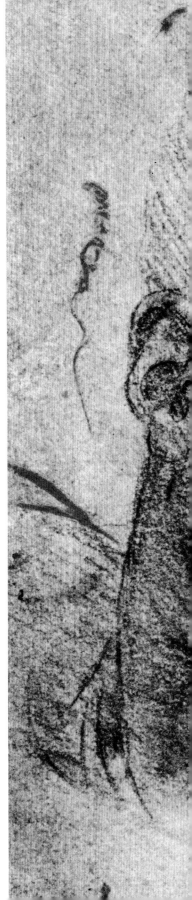

Leonardo da Vinci
**Study of Heads for
The Battle of Anghiari**
1503–1505
Silverpoint, black charcoal,
and red chalk on paper
7.52 x 7.4 inches
(19.1 x 18.8 cm)
National Museum, Budapest

standard, which has been grasped by a soldier, who seeks by the strength of his shoulders, as he spurs his horse to flight, having turned his body backwards and seized the staff of the standard, to wrest it by force from the hands of four others, of whom two are defending it, each with one hand, and raising their swords in the other, are trying to sever the staff; while an old soldier in a red cap, crying out, grips the staff with one hand, and raising a scimitar with the other, furiously aims a blow in order to cut off both the hands of those who, gnashing their teeth in the struggle, are striving in attitudes of the utmost fierceness to defend their banner; besides which, on the ground, between the legs of the horses, there are two figures in foreshortening that are fighting together, and the one on the ground has over him a soldier who has raised his arm as high as possible, that thus with greater force he may plunge a dagger into his throat, in order to end his life; while the other, struggling with his legs and arms, is doing what he can to escape death.

"It is not possible to describe the invention that Leonardo showed in the garments of the soldiers, all varied by him in different ways, and likewise in the helmet-crests and other ornaments; not to mention the incredible mastery that he displayed in the forms and lineaments of the horses, which Leonardo, with their fiery spirit, muscles, and shapely beauty, drew better than any other master" (p. 637).

The copies of *The Fight for the Standard* are the only records that have come down to us of some of Leonardo's work for the Palazzo Vecchio. One of the most famous of these is known as the *Tavola Doria*, or Doria Panel (Alte

Right:
Leonardo da Vinci
**Study of Combatants on
Horseback and on Foot
for The Battle of Anghiari**
1503–1504
Pen and ink on paper
6.3 x 5.98 inches
(16 x 15.2 cm)
Accademia, Venice

Following pages:
Leonardo da Vinci
**Study of Combatants on
Horseback and on Foot
for The Battle of Anghiari**
1503–1504
Pen and ink on paper
5.71 x 5.98 inches
(14.5 x 15.2 cm)
Accademia, Venice

Pinakothek, Munich), done by an anonymous artist around 1504. As for the cartoon, a part—perhaps the central section that was actually painted—was left in the Great Council Chamber, while the rest was abandoned by the artist in his studio at Santa Maria Novella when he stopped work sometime between the end of 1505 and the beginning of 1506. Nothing further is known about either drawing. Another of the most famous copies—a copy of a copy—is a drawing by Peter Paul Rubens (Musée du Louvre, Paris). This conveys just how far Leonardo's conception diverged from the traditional representations of battle; it is conceived as an overwhelming vortex of action that spreads outward from the central group of *The Fight for the Standard*, and displays an unheard-of range of gestures and poses. This is what primarily distinguishes the work of Leonardo from that of Michelangelo, who was concerned with the virtuoso depiction of male bodies, and showed the Florentine soldiers surprised as they bathe in a river by the unexpected attack of their enemies.

In Leonardo's many surviving sketches for *The Battle of Anghiari*, drawings of other subjects also appear on the same sheets. One of particular importance shows a rearing horse; nearby is a female nude with some little children, repeated in several versions. The figure of the kneeling woman relates to the *Leda*, a lost painting for which there is much direct and indirect surviving evidence. This includes some studies by Leonardo of heads and hairstyles, of which the best-known is the *Head of Leda* now in the Windsor Castle collection. Written references to the work come to us from the Anonimo Gaddiano and the artist and scholar Gian Paolo Lomazzo, both of whom mention a nude figure of Leda by Leonardo, using similar descriptive terms. Little is known of this work; the only certain thing is that Leonardo sketched the *Leda* in pencil during his second Florentine period, presumably around 1504, and that he finished the work after he returned to Milan. In the first sketches the idea was to represent the figure in a kneeling pose, but the artist revised his concept in a new, standing version, probably in Milan.

From the moment he returned to Florence, Leonardo once again became an essential reference point for the artists of his era, as we may surmise from the degree of interest they evinced in his works. Both *The Battle of Anghiari* and the *Leda* were the object of much study and many copies, attracting the attention of numerous painters. Two reconstructions are particularly outstanding: One is the Spiridon *Leda*, now in Vinci at the Museo Leonardiano (Museum of Leonardo), which at one time was considered by some scholars to be by the hand of the master; the other is in the Borghese Gallery in Rome, and is the work of the painter Giovanni Bazzi, known as il Sodoma.

Leonardo's immediate contribution to Florence's new artistic spring was in the great potential for innovation that his works presented, which younger

Preceding pages:
Anonymous
Fight for the Standard
copy after Leonardo's *Battle of Anghiari*, 16th century
Palazzo Vecchio, Florence

Opposite:
Leonardo da Vinci
Study of a Rearing Horse
1503–1504
Red chalk and lapis [lead] on paper, 6.02 x 5.59 inches (15.3 x 14.2 cm)
Royal Library, Windsor

artists were quick to embrace and build upon, responding to the fresh spirit. In Florence, in particular, the leaders of this younger generation gave impetus to a renewed direction for painting, thanks to the close attention they paid to the great masters who had preceded them: Raphael, Leonardo, and Michelangelo. Andrea del Sarto, Pontormo, and Rosso Fiorentino were among the first to signal the change that was occurring in the artistic and cultural landscape, stamped with an anticlassical taste that was expressed in entirely individual terms.

The legacy of Leonardo is not only his extraordinary work but also in his thoughts and reflections on the nature of art itself. In his *Treatise on Painting* he wrote, "The musician says that his science is equal in stature to that of the painter because it joins together a body made up of many members." Leonardo emphasized the parallels between a painter's conception of the integration of the body's members and that of the musician concerning musical notes: "Music, in its harmonic intervals, makes its suave melodies, which are composed from varied notes. . . . [and] the harmonic proportionality of painting is composed simultaneously from various components." In both cases, harmony must be achieved, whether in a single figure or in a whole composition, so it is necessary to maintain a constant, dynamic interplay of rhythms and associations among individual parts. We see this process of integration of discrete parts in the *Saint Anne* cartoon, and it must have been the basis of *The Battle of Anghiari*, as best we can determine.

As has been noted, Vasari mentioned 1503 as the year Leonardo began one of his most famous works, the *Mona Lisa*, although the date of the work remains debatable. In June 1506 Leonardo left the Palazzo Vecchio painting unfinished in order to return to Milan, whither he had been bidden by Charles d'Amboise, the legate of the French king and ruler of Milan, promising to return to Tuscany within three months. But his residency in Milan lasted longer than he had anticipated, until September 1507. The following year, he did return once more to Florence, as a guest in the house of Pietro di Braccio Martelli, and lent his support to a project by the sculptor Giovan Francesco Rustici for a bronze figure group intended for the Baptistery. But on September 12, 1508, we have a record of his presence in Milan again, and there he remained, except for brief periods, until 1513.

Above:
Leonardo da Vinci
Study for the Head of Leda
ca. 1503–1507
Black charcoal, pen, and ink on paper, 6.97 x 5.79 inches (17.7 x 14.7 cm)
Royal Library, Windsor

Opposite:
Giovanni Bazzi, known as Il Sodoma
Leda
copy after Leonardo
early 16th century
Borghese Gallery, Rome

Above and opposite:
Giovanni Bazzi,
known as Il Sodoma
Leda
copy after Leonardo
(details)

THE MONA LISA

"Leonardo undertook to execute, for Francesco del Giocondo, the portrait of Mona Lisa, his wife; and after toiling over it for four years, he left it unfinished; and the work is now in the collection of King Frances of France, at Fontainebleau" (p. 635). With these words Vasari began to describe the history of the most celebrated painting of all time, underscoring its complex origins ("toiling over it for four years") and the incomplete state in which Leonardo left it ("he left it unfinished"). Actually, this last assertion is contradicted by another source: the account, dated October 10, 1517, of a visit by Antonio de Beatis, secretary to Cardinal Luigi of Aragon, to Leonardo's French studio at Cloux. De Beatis records that he saw three paintings at Leonardo's, a "Saint John the Baptist," a "Madonna and Child," and finally, "a portrait of a certain Florentine lady done from life." He calls all of them "most perfect," that is, finished. Equally uncertain is the date of the work, which Leonardo must have begun almost contemporaneously with *The Battle of Anghiari*, that is, around 1504, since Raphael knew the painting. He punctiliously reproduced its pose in his *Portrait of Maddalena Doni* (Pitti Palace, Florence) and in part in the *Cowper Madonna* (National Gallery of Art, Washington, D.C.); both works are datable to 1505. This does not necessarily prove that the *Mona Lisa* was finished at that date, but suggests that the painting was already well-known in Florence

at the beginning of the sixteenth century, although it was probably still incomplete—or rather, existed in a version that was not yet definitive. In fact, we may infer from Vasari that Leonardo almost certainly returned to the *Mona Lisa* several times. A confirmation of this lies in the complex development of the landscape behind the sitter, which is associated with studies of atmospheric agents (e.g., wind and clouds) and the stratification of rock formations that Leonardo began only in the second decade of the century.

Another unresolved problem is that of the lady's identity. Scholars do not universally consider Vasari reliable on the *Mona Lisa*'s attribution; some have, from time to time, identified the portrait as that of Isabella d'Este, Pacifica Brandano, or Isabella Gualanda—the latter two courtesans who moved in the circle of Giuliano de' Medici. Recently, the historian Giuseppe Pallanti has conducted painstaking archival research to reexamine in depth Vasari's famous identification of the sitter as Lisa Gherardini, wife of Francesco del Giocondo; he has meticulously reconstructed the life and family history of the noblewoman. Freed from the almost legendary status conferred on her by the fame of the painting, she emerges in his description as a real, three-dimensional person. One explanation for why we continue to find it difficult to identify the sitter is the plausible hypothesis that Leonardo did not create a

126

"portrait from life" this time, but worked to distance himself progressively from the subject—whomever she might have been—in order, gradually, to develop a "universal" portrait. In other words, the *Mona Lisa*, far from strictly reproducing the factual features of one individual person, is essentially schematic and symbolic: an archetype of representation.

In the *Mona Lisa* Leonardo painted the "portrait" par excellence: not simply an individual portrait, but a representation that, deliberately freed from every specific and superfluous attribute, becomes a universal image, almost an icon. As such, the work is a sort of compendium of all of Leonardo's poetics: a *summa* of all the art theories he developed, supported by his parallel research in other fields. For example, the delicate rendering of light, which plays across the lady's face in vibrant, gradual brushstrokes so as to suggest the idea of imperceptible movement, can only be explained in terms of Leonardo's studies of the refraction of light on colored bodies. In this figure, caught in three-quarter view and turning slightly toward the viewer, Leonardo succeeded as never before in harmonizing action and feeling in a "psychological" exploration that he began in his earliest portraits and pursued throughout his career. In this sense there is a perfect accord between the original interlacing of the woman's hands, a clever device halfway between a casual gesture and an artificially formal pose, and her vague expression, whose indefinite gaze seems to encompass many emotions without expressing any one specifically. The artist sought harmonious coherence on many levels in this painting. Figure and background are fused with meticulous balance, so that the landscape extends several of the figure's directional lines (i.e., sight lines): the sinuous curves of the river echoing those of her bosom, a slight slope falling behind the line of her left shoulder, the mountains that do not rise above the level of her gaze.

Acclaimed, copied, celebrated, and satirized, the *Mona Lisa* has always exerted an irresistible fascination, only partly attributable to the veil of mystery that surrounds her; above all, it is the acknowledged extraordinariness of the picture, in which Leonardo most brilliantly confirmed his own undisputed genius, that confers the exceptional fame the work enjoys today, five centuries after its creation.

Leonardo da Vinci
Mona Lisa (detail)

Chapter 4
The Final Years: Between Milan, Rome, and France

In 1508 Leonardo was once again summoned to Milan, which had been under French rule since 1500, when the army of Louis XII had captured it. The governor of Milan, Charles d'Amboise, Count of Chaumont, wished to avail himself of Leonardo's eclectic talents, and asked the republic's chief magistrate, Pier Soderini to send him from Florence. The count's principal aim was to revive the city's renowned tradition of patronage, established under Ludovico il Moro. Because Leonardo had personally contributed to the prestige of the Sforza capital in the previous decade through his creation of certain famous masterworks, in the eyes of Amboise a new project by the Tuscan master was indispensable to his ambitions.

Oddly, an equestrian statue was again one of the first projects with which Leonardo was occupied upon his return to Milan. This had a curious copycat quality, following upon the failure of the plans for the monument to Francesco Sforza many years earlier. This time he was commissioned to create a sculptural group portraying Gian Giacomo Trivulzio, the Italian *condottiere*, or freelance military captain, in the service of the French who had wrested Milan from Ludovico. The work was to be placed in the Church of San Nazaro in Milan, in a mausoleum designed by Bramantino and built in 1512. The fate of this statue seemed to echo that of its predecessor: A series of careful studies and preparatory drawings were made, but the Trivulzio monument was never cast, and Leonardo once again saw his plans for this project come to naught. Nevertheless, in the numerous sketches relating to this work, most of which are in the Royal Collection at Windsor, we see clearly how Leonardo avoided mechanically repeating the same compositional schema as in his previous effort, turning instead to a logical, careful reconsideration of the themes he had addressed earlier, from the motif of the prancing horse to the precise study of how the animal moved at a trot, explored in myriad variations. But it was in the overall plan of the work that Leonardo completely broke away from his design for the Sforza monument. This time he imagined an elaborate sculptural group in which the *condottiere* on horseback, shown in several sketches wrapped in a large cloak, is the

Leonardo da Vinci
The Virgin of the Rocks
(second version)
ca. 1495–1508 (detail)
Oil on canvas
74.61 x 47.24 inches
(189.5 x 120 cm)
National Gallery, London

131

crowning figure of a cleverly designed arched structure, with four figures at the base supporting the upper register.

It was in Leonardo's nature to be fascinated by every sphere of human knowledge, and he did not limit his research to the study of sculpture, but took advantage of this second visit to the Lombard city to explore other fields of inquiry and thus to find further means to broaden his expertise. Above all, the scientific study of natural resources led him, after painstaking observation of the principles of hydrodynamics and geology, to propose concrete answers to the problem of Milan's water supply. A series of precise, rigorously annotated plans for the building and use of hydraulic machinery, for the construction of canals and locks, and for a bold plan to widen the Adda River, with a minutely detailed topographical map, all date to this period. At the same time, Leonardo formed a close, collaborative friendship with Marcantonio della Torre, an anatomist at the University of Pavia, through whom he was able to study the structure and functions of the human body more deeply, to examine dissected corpses directly, and to make drawings of them in his notebooks. Now Leonardo's drawing reached a new level of virtuosity; it became a true instrument of scientific inquiry and an effective means of investigating every aspect of human physiology in order to understand the laws governing the function and interconnections of bones, tendons, and muscles.

In conjunction with these projects, Leonardo also managed to pursue his studies of architecture, for example matching the study of the mechanics of water with an exploration of the design of gardens and parks. Thus his plans for a suburban villa commissioned by Charles d'Amboise include a generous area of gardens, enlivened by numerous fountains and pools. Unfortunately, when the governor of Milan died suddenly in 1511 this plan met the same fate as so many of Leonardo's other projects. Another architectural scheme of these years was the restoration of Villa Melzi in Vaprio d'Adda, where the artist stayed in 1513. The designs for this last work, however, seem to be purely theoretical and cannot be correlated with any actual architectural reconstruction of the building.

Definitely more concrete are the results Leonardo achieved in the field of painting in these years, above all in the documented completion of some works that had previously been left at the idea stage, existing only in preparatory drawings. One of the works to which Leonardo returned in these years was the *Leda*, a work now unfortunately lost, whose preliminary studies, as we have seen, sometimes appear on the same sheet of sketches with drawings for *The Battle of Anghiari*. It is not possible to know what the painting looked like in its final form, but a few partial glimpses may be found in some autograph drawings and in copies made by artists in Leonardo's circle. These, in turn, exhibit numerous variations in details. However, it seems probable that after first

Opposite:
Leonardo da Vinci
Study for the Trivulzio Monument
1513
Red chalk and ink on paper
8.9 x 6.93 inches
(22.6 x 17.6 cm)
Royal Library, Windsor

Following pages:
Leonardo da Vinci
Studies for the Trivulzio Monument
1508–1510 (details)
Pen and ink on paper
11.02 x 7.8 inches
(28 x 19.8 cm)
Royal Library, Windsor

49

134

imagining a kneeling *Leda* (as in the sketch done during the *Battle of Anghiari* period), Leonardo modified the figure's pose a good deal in the final version, transforming the *Leda* into a graceful standing figure, as seen in surviving copies.

Consequently, as he worked on the painting, he drew progressively more and more on classical statuary for his models. This may be seen in the balanced posture of the standing *Leda* in workshop copies, which closely resembles the pose found in standing figures in the great Greco-Roman sculptural tradition. In the autograph drawing of the head of *Leda*, Leonardo again demonstrates a surprising originality, joined with a masterly command of plastic modeling derived from the study of classical monuments. In the delicate tilt of her head and her discreetly downturned gaze, the mythical mother of Castor and Pollux recalls the grace of certain ancient Roman sculptures. The extremely intricate hairstyle, which Leonardo reproduced precisely in a later version as well, is the fruit of the artist's incessant inventiveness.

The other, more famous work to which Leonardo returned during this, his second Milan period, is the panel of *Saint Anne, the Virgin, and Child with the Lamb* (Musée du Louvre, Paris) a theme that we have seen him visit, albeit with distinct differences, in the cartoon in the National Gallery, London.

Compared with that preparatory drawing—which, we recall, should be considered a work in itself, independent of this later reconsideration of the same theme—the Louvre painting abolishes the figure of the child Saint John, substituting a little lamb, symbol of the Passion, which the Christ Child is consciously reaching to embrace. The definite impression of undulating movement conveyed by the powerful disequilibrium of the Virgin and Child is mirrored in the water visible in the upper register of the work and is undoubtedly connected to the studies Leonardo made based on studies of figures in motion that he had completed while he was working out the agitated scene of *The Battle of Anghiari*.

The most natural consequence of the artist's return to Milan was the influence of his extremely personal style on a circle of local artists, some of whom had already had contact with him during his first Milanese period. Moreover, Leonardo's return to Milan seems to have reinvigorated the artistic efforts of this group of students, although not all of them were able to overcome a certain stylistic provincialism. Among those who took up Leonardesque themes and whose work stands out were Ambrogio de' Predis, Leonardo's close collaborator; Giovanni Marco d'Oggiono, Antonio Boltraffio, Bernardino Luini, and Salai, mentioned earlier; and Cesare da Sesto and Andrea Solario. These last two developed an adaptation of Leonardo's style, and this updating of his pictorial innovations enriched their own style in interesting ways. In particular, Cesare da Sesto, whose work acquired a reputation beyond local circles, demonstrated an

Leonardo da Vinci
Study for Saint Anne, the Virgin, and Child with the Lamb
ca. 1501–1506
Lead point, pen, and ink on paper
Accademia, Venice

Leonardo da Vinci
Study for Saint Anne
ca. 1500
Charcoal on paper
Royal Library, Windsor

SAINT ANNE, THE VIRGIN, AND CHILD WITH THE LAMB

Although Leonardo completed this work during the last phase of his second sojourn in Milan—that is, around 1510—he probably began it in the first years of the sixteenth century, as some preparatory studies of heads and draperies suggest. In any case, the dating question is only one of several problems surrounding the *Saint Anne*, among the most controversial of all his artworks. The painting that "went to France," according to an unnamed chronicler known as the Anonimo Gaddiano, writing around 1540, must be this celebrated version, which differs compositionally from a cartoon of the same subject now in the National Gallery in London. After the artist's death, the painting was inherited by one of his students, Francesco Melzi, and was sent back to Italy from the artist's French studio in the chateau of Cloux, along with several codices and other paintings that formed a part of his estate. After Melzi's death, around 1570, we have no further news of the panel for many years, but it was probably sold when most of Leonardo's estate was dispersed. In 1629–1630, during the war for Mantua, the French troops of Cardinal Richelieu traced it to Casale Monferrato, in Piedmont; in 1636, on Richelieu's orders, it came into the possession of King Louis XIII and thence into the French royal collections, until its final transfer to the Louvre in 1810.

In the London cartoon the figures are organized in a single, compact group. In contrast to that tight structure, this version presents the figures discretely, using a calculated dynamism, especially in the dramatically off-balance pose of the Virgin. The resulting strong diagonal draws the eye down along her extended arms to the lamb. The figure of Saint Anne, seated behind the others, is markedly massive. Leonardo froze her in a pose that is almost the mirror image of the trajectory of the other figures, emphasizing the deliberate instability of the whole group. He used several devices to create a sense of enveloping vertigo: setting the saint's face against a distant, remote, and curiously almost glacial landscape, veiled in a thick mist and counterposing unexpected glints of light with passages of intense shadow. And yet the well-contrived spatial structure and the original, contrasting construction of the group of figures seem almost insignificant compared with some moments of poignant tenderness, especially the melancholy gaze of Mary, in which Leonardo captures her intensely maternal, human fear for the fate of her child.

Left, with details on
the following pages:
Leonardo da Vinci
**Saint Anne, the
Virgin, and Child
with the Lamb**
ca. 1501–1510
Oil on panel
66.14 x 51.18 inches
(168 x 130 cm)
Musée du Louvre,
Paris

artistic awareness of Leonardo's ideas that rises above a slavish repetition of the most easily imitated elements of his painting. His works also show a singular attention to the work of artists such as Raphael, Baldassare Peruzzi, and il Sodoma; yet he was able to develop a very personal language, easily identifiable even when he was merely copying works by Leonardo. One example is his interpretation of the *Leda* (Uffizi Gallery, Florence), one of several known versions of the original, which was unfortunately lost in the seventeenth century. The painting is based on the Greek myth of Leda, the Spartan queen who was seduced by the god Zeus in the guise of a swan, and who gave birth to two sets of twins. Cesare da Sesto's version offers a slight variation that is absent from other copies and therefore most likely his own addition to Leonardo's work. Other versions (one in Rome at the Borghese Gallery, another in a private collection in Salisbury, England) depict the moment when Leda proudly shows her children to the swan; in the Uffizi version the babies are newborn and jump out of their just-broken eggshells: Castor and Pollux, Helen and Clytemnestra.

A work that was probably conceived by Leonardo but possibly executed or completed by his students is the *Madonna and Child with a Yarn-Winder*, also called *The Madonna of the Spindle* (private collection, New York). As such, it offers a case study in collaboration between the master and his followers. First mentioned in 1501 in a letter from Fra' Pietro da Novellara, vicar general of the Carmelite monastic order, to the Marchioness Isabella d'Este, the *Madonna and Child with a Yarn-Winder* seems entirely to lack that studied interiority typical of Leonardo's figures, while the mountainous landscape, which is similar to that in the *Saint Anne* and the *Mona Lisa*, does not display the same dexterity in blending the figures harmoniously with their background.

Pietro da Novellara offers a possible explanation: He confirms that Leonardo, who usually had a great many ongoing commissions and projects, often allowed his students to finish his paintings, limiting his involvement to supervising the various phases of work and occasionally taking up a brush himself. That may have been the case in this work, which exists in several other versions, suggesting that its iconography was well liked by both artists and buyers.

Another important fact to bear in mind concerning Leonardo's working method in these years is the undeniable change in his way of depicting the natural landscape, which can be seen with particular clarity when works of the late 1400s are compared with those painted twenty years later. It is difficult to establish how much his increasing interest in the study of antiquity, which grew stronger over the years, influenced this change in style; the fact remains that Leonardo's artistic trajectory followed two paths—the exploration of nature and the investigation of classical models—and the two interacted and intertwined on many levels, merging into a single, reciprocal relationship of cause and effect.

Cesare da Sesto
Leda
copy after Leonardo
ca. 1508–1515
Uffizi Gallery, Florence

Above and opposite:
Cesare da Sesto
Leda (details)

146

But just what is this shift in Leonardo's approach to the representation of nature? The general view is that the artist gradually became more interested in reproducing certain natural events, with a particular predilection for metamorphic phenomena, such as geological stratifications, the formation of clouds and fog, and the fluid properties of water. In all these sorts of studies, Leonardo showed a growing taste for schematic depictions of form; he repeated modular graphic marks almost obsessively, often in vortex patterns, to depict vapors, cliffs, waves, and currents, as he searched for an ever-greater effect of dynamism. Leonardo expressed this sort of formal simplification in terms of pure intellectual development; that is, he aimed not simply to record a phenomenon, but also to develop a much more complex creative process, using a schematic graphic language. Leonardo's vision of nature, probably influenced by his desire to address the classical concept of art, now revealed so profound a grasp of its laws that he recreated a sort of "parallel" nature, made of phenomena that he had not investigated directly, but revised mentally.

Such a change in approach was bound to appear in the works of these years, foremost in the second version of *The Virgin of the Rocks* (National Gallery, London), which Leonardo probably completed between 1507 and 1508. In this second interpretation of the same subject as the Louvre panel, he varied the composition in some details, for example removing the gesture and altering the gaze of the angel who now no longer looks at the viewer or points to the infant Saint John—details that created a certain ambiguity of meaning in the first version. Another difference is in the relationship of the figures to the landscape context. In the London panel, the rocky peaks behind the group rise to fill the entire top half of the painting, reinforcing their architectonic function and pushing the figures forward, closer to the picture plane. Scholars have detected the hands of Leonardo's students—perhaps Boltraffio or Marco d'Oggiono—in the execution of the figures, which are presented more monumentally than in the first version, so that although they are set in the same compositional scheme as before, they now make the background recede further into the distance. But it is the transformation in the treatment of light and the unique rendering of atmosphere that make the London *Virgin of the Rocks* more than a mere replica of the earlier version. This alteration in ambience is the result of Leonardo's more modern approach to the depiction of natural landscape: The bodies of the figures are illumined by a new light, sharp and cool, which also strikes the steep surfaces of the crags and reveals their complex morphological structure. The painting is fragmented into closely observed, well-defined zones of deep shadow and accentuated light. Precise tonal correspondences offset the spatial gap between

Right:
Leonardo da Vinci
and collaborators
**Madonna and Child
with a Yarn-Winder**
ca. 1501
Oil on panel,
transferred to canvas
19.76 x 14.33 inches
(50.2 x 36.4 cm)
Private Collection, New York

Page 150
School of Leonardo
**Madonna and Child
with a Yarn-Winder**
Oil on panel
19.02 x 14.53 inches
(48.3 x 36.9 cm)
Drumlanrig Castle, Scotland
(stolen in 2003)

Page 151
School of Leonardo
**Madonna and Child
with a Yarn-Winder**
National Gallery of Scotland,
Edinburgh

figures and ground, which are united by numerous strong light reflections, adding to the intense sense of sacredness in the scene, which assumes the dimensions of a distant, supernatural event.

Leonardo's Milanese sojourn ended in 1513, possibly precipitated by the uncertain political situation, which had been complicated by the Sforzas' return to power the previous year. He accepted the invitation of Giuliano de' Medici, his new patron, to return to Rome, a city he had visited at the beginning of the century, during the pontificate of Julius II. When Julius died in 1513, Giovanni de' Medici, son of Lorenzo the Magnificent and brother of Giuliano, was elected pope, taking the name Leo X. Like his predecessor, he made cultural development of the city a primary goal of his rule, and to that end commissioned works from all the greatest artists of the day. Leonardo joined many of the other prominent artists of the Italian Renaissance there: Michelangelo, who had completed the great Sistine Chapel frescoes and was now working on the monumental tomb for Julius II; Raphael, who had been appointed architect of the Fabbrica di San Pietro, the agency responsible for maintaining the Vatican buildings, was also now under commission to decorate a pair of Vatican chambers, the Stanze Vaticane. The Rome that welcomed Leonardo was in the midst of a period of exceptional artistic splendor; despite the grave political and religious problems Leo X faced—the Protestant Reformation on the one hand and the expansionist appetites of Emperor Charles V on the other—the years of his pontificate were distinguished by the creation of supreme masterpieces of art, marking him as a patron of exceptional ability.

In this climate of cultural ferment, befitting his own ingenious versatility, Leonardo threw himself into a number of projects at once, ranging casually from urban planning to military engineering, from the study of classical statuary to mathematics—obviously without abandoning the fundamental practice of painting. Among his projects of this time in Rome were plans, developed with Giovanni Scotti of Como, to drain the nearby Pontine marshes, acquired in 1515 by Giuliano de' Medici at the request of his brother, Leo X. He also reorganized the port of Civitavecchia, for which he designed a structure, never built, probably inspired by the placement of the wharf in the ancient Roman era; curiously, the same task had earlier been assigned to Bramante, who, like Leonardo, worked as a painter and architect in both Sforza's Milan and the Rome of Julius II.

A remarkable painting, *Saint John the Baptist* (Musée du Louvre, Paris), probably belongs to this Roman period. It may originally have been painted as a commission for the *Confraternità di San Giovanni* (Confraternity of Saint John) there. But in 1517 the panel was still in Leonardo's studio, as the diplomat Antonio de Beatis noted in his account of his visit to Leonardo in October of that

Leonardo da Vinci
The Virgin of the Rocks
(second version)
ca. 1507–1508
Oil on canvas
74.61 x 47.24 inches
(189.5 x 120 cm)
National Gallery, London

year, along with the *Saint Anne* and a "portrait" identifiable as the *Mona Lisa*. The date of the painting is undetermined: some scholars place it as early as the second Florentine period, noting that John is that city's patron saint. A later date is suggested by the treatment of the saint's hair, whose distinctive spiral curls recall those "vertical motions" often seen in Leonardo's later studies of whirlpools, storms, and other spiral forms. In other words, the long, dramatic ringlets that tumble to the saint's shoulders use the same expressive visual language Leonardo employed in his highly personal renderings of natural phenomena; these did not inform his work until his second Milan period.

Aside from the problematic date of the painting, Leonardo's peculiar interpretation of *Saint John the Baptist* has provoked considerable and varied critical commentary. The saint is depicted in half-bust, turning slightly to the left, but gazing directly at the viewer; the prominent upward gesture of the right arm, which terminates the serpentine line of the composition, creates a marked diagonal that is counterposed to a second diagonal formed by the tilted head and the left arm. But beyond the elegance of the composition, Leonardo inserted

Above:
View of the Stanza della Segnatura with the frescoes of Raphael, 1508–1511 Vatican Museums, Rome

Opposite:
View of the Sistine Chapel with the frescoes of Michelangelo, 1508–1512 Vatican Museums, Rome

some extremely ambiguous, unconventional elements into the painting: The feminine features of the face, which can practically be superimposed on those of the Louvre *Saint Anne*; the disturbing expression of winking complicity; and the equally lascivious leopard pelt worn by the saint all function to detach the figure from traditional canons of sacred images, turning it instead into a kind of pagan divinity.

A related work, the *Bacchus* (Musée du Louvre, Paris), was probably painted in the same period and has some significant analogies to the *Saint John*. Scholars have mostly agreed to seeing the hands of assistants in this panel, which originally was to have represented Saint John in the desert, and indeed is often referred to by that name in the documentary sources, which in some cases provide such detailed descriptions of the subject that it cannot be mistaken for another work. Although Leonardo may have intended to depict a sacred subject, he included the same ambiguities that appeared in the *Saint John the Baptist* and added a classicizing pose and a landscape, elements that depart from more traditional representations of the theme. These disturbing details may have provoked the later addition of elements that transformed the painting from a *Saint John* into a *Bacchus*: The vine leaves in his hair, the thyrsus (the staff of Bacchus), and the panther pelt are traditional attributes of the classical god and were probably added in the seventeenth century to weaken an improper reading of the subject as *Saint John*, converting it from a Christian to a mythological scene. Leaving aside these complexities, the conception of the work is securely attributable to Leonardo, as evidenced by the articulate pose of the figure, which echoes that often found in classical sculpture, and by the relationship of figure to landscape background, set in stronger light than the rest of the painting. The ambiguous fascination of the Bacchus and the delicacy of features that it shares with the *Saint John the Baptist*, are themselves indications of its authorship by Leonardo.

After the death of his patron, Giuliano de' Medici, in 1516, Leonardo left Rome and moved to France for reasons that are not entirely clear. He went to the court of Francis I, who admired him greatly. The French king's appreciation for the Tuscan artist, which has been much romanticized in later descriptions, was nonetheless sincere and strong: Leonardo was immediately given the title of "first painter, engineer, and architect" to the king. Housed in the chateau of Cloux at Amboise and granted a lavish pension and various privileges, the master turned to many different tasks, despite his now advanced age and the difficulties resulting from the progressive paralysis from which he suffered. He continued to show the same multifaceted capacity to work in many different fields, as he had done during his years at the most important courts of Italy. Leonardo's interest in hydrology, for example, seems only to have grown:

Opposite, with detail
on the following pages:
Leonardo da Vinci
Saint John the Baptist
ca. 1514
Oil on panel
27.17 x 22.44 inches
(69 x 57 cm)
Musée du Louvre, Paris

263

Left:
Leonardo da Vinci
Young Bacchus
Drawing on paper
6.7 x 5.12 inches
(17 x 13 cm)
Accademia, Venice

Opposite, with detail
on the following pages:
Leonardo da Vinci
and collaborator
Bacchus
ca. 1514
Oil on panel,
transferred to canvas
69.7 x 45.28 inches
(177 x 115 cm)
Musée du Louvre, Paris

He proposed a bold project to unite France's Loire and Saône Rivers, in order to link France's outlet into the Atlantic with that in the Mediterranean. In his innovative project for the royal chateau of Romorantin (never carried out), the artist designed not only the expansion of the royal residence but also a detailed scheme of canals to feed fountains and artificial pools where aquatic tournaments and mock sea battles could be staged. He further served as designer of temporary theatrical machinery and stage sets, costumes, and decorations for court galas and festivities, among them the baptism of the dauphin. And at this late stage of his mature thought, he delved deeply into the exploration of an astonishing new theme in a key group of drawings that stand as the final recorded evidence of his exceptional creative power. Thus began the remarkable series of *Deluge* drawings in which the artist, fascinated almost to the point of obsession by a vision of natural catastrophe, generated a

View of the Chateau of Cloux at Amboise, France

Jean Clouet
**Portrait of Francis I,
King of France**
ca. 1530
Musée du Louvre, Paris

dramatic representation of calamities: rockslides, earthquakes, and floods whose tragic qualities are belied by the lightness of the compositions and the fineness of the execution. The king must have asked him to produce some paintings, too, but as his illness continued to worsen, so that according to de Beatis his right hand was completely paralyzed, he was prevented from creating new masterpieces.

Attended by Francesco Melzi and Salai, former students who had followed him to France, Leonardo died in Amboise on May 2, 1519, bequeathing to them most of the works still in his possession. Thus the extraordinary artistic path of this unique personality came to a close at the court of Francis I. Leonardo was a genius without precedent, universally recognized, whose limitless and enduring fame is the only possible monument to his legendary talent, which no definition can fully encompass.

Chapter 5
The Myth of Leonardo

The uniqueness and greatness of Leonardo's art have always been recognized. That is, he did not have to await that critical reevaluation that artists of the past must often undergo before they join the pantheon of art history's protagonists. From his earliest days as a simple apprentice in Verrocchio's workshop, Leonardo had shown that he had innate, extraordinary capacities of mind and hand, which were just waiting for the opportunity to take form and express themselves. Anyone wishing to write or speak of Leonardo, therefore, must start by describing him as a "universal genius," an incomparable example of the perfect marriage of art and science, an unflagging experimenter in every field of human knowledge. It is the extraordinary range of interests to which he turned his genius that renders him truly unique—and not only in the realm of painting, or even of art in general. Leonardo examined nature and the material world as they are and as they appear, exploring every element of them and every law determining their existence, and becoming expert in their study. Thus he was also a mathematician, geometer, astronomer, philosopher, geologist, poet, musician, and, naturally, a painter.

All this fit within the contemporary Renaissance conception of knowledge, in which art and science were not two distinct fields, but were reciprocally interconnected. Leonardo had to adopt the methodologies of the scientist in order to represent the material world, just as he needed to use the instruments of art to transmit his own knowledge in the clearest way possible. This idea forms the basis for Leonardo's claim that painting is first among the sciences. Like all of the creative disciplines, painting must first investigate and know the laws of nature, but more than any other art, it possesses a power to communicate with all, without requiring any sort of translation or mediation. For Leonardo, the principal purpose of painting was to render visually things as they exist—not just their mere appearances, but as a variegated universe of proportional relationships, optical variations, and psychological and emotional motivations.

In his *Treatise on Painting*, he wrote: "The divinity of the science of painting considers works both human and divine, which are bounded by surfaces, that is to say the boundary lines of bodies, with which she dictates to the sculptor the

Leonardo da Vinci
Self-Portrait
ca. 1503
Red chalk on paper
13.11 x 8.39 inches
(33.3 x 21.3 cm)
Royal Library, Turin

way to perfect his statues. Through her principle, that is to say, draughtsmanship, she teaches the architect how to make his buildings convey pleasure to the eye; she teaches the potters about the varieties of vases, and also the goldsmiths, the weavers and the embroiderers. She has invented the characters in which the various languages are expressed; she has given numerals to the mathematicians; she has shown figurative representation to geometry; she has taught the students of optics, the perspective painters, the astrologers, the technicians, the engineers, the builders of buildings and the constructors of machines."

Painting is thus a science, and one cannot have science without knowledge. Leonardo *knew* because he *investigated*; he ceaselessly studied all that was available to his eyes in order to translate it brilliantly into paintings, seeking to transfer into the painted work that same visual perception to which his eye was privy. From such assumptions was born his celebrated *sfumato* technique; the progressive erasure of outlines served to immerse every element of a composition in a single, enveloping atmosphere, reconstructing in paint the experience of the human eye as it observes external reality. At the same time, Leonardo insisted on the importance of studying those "motions of the mind" without which no human action can occur. His eye simultaneously observed inwardly and outwardly, an absolutely unheard-of innovation in the fifteenth century—unrepeatable, perhaps, even in our own time. All of his explorations passed through the filter of drawing, evidenced in the famous "Codices," in which he collected innumerable notes and studies conducted in the most varied fields over the course of his life as an artist-scientist. The varying fortunes of these notebooks after his death bear witness to the value given to his every exploration.

But every new critical assessment of Leonardo can only add its might to the wealth of praise that has been written about this genius and handed down for generations—beginning, indeed, when he was still alive and working. He was already mythic during his own lifetime—a myth fed continually by new confirmations of his exceptionality. In Milan, at the court of Ludovico il Moro, the poet Bernardo Bellincioni described his versatile genius enthusiastically, recalling the decorations that Leonardo had created for Bellincioni's theater piece, the famous "Feast of Paradise." The performance, which took place on the occasion of the wedding of Gian Galeazzo Sforza and Isabella of Aragon in 1490, was a sort of theatrical event based on mythological themes, for which, "with great ingenuity and art, the Florentine Maestro Leonardo da Vinci constructed a Paradise complete with seven planets that revolved, and the planets were played by men." In 1493 Bellincioni published a cycle of poems, the *Rime*, or *Rhymes*, that contributed greatly to the creation of the Leonardo myth: "A new Apelles has come from Florence," he wrote in a margin note to a

commentary on the poem. This comparison with the greatest painter of antiquity was repeated by Vasari, who quoted the poet Giovan Battista Strozzi: "And so, on account of all his qualities, so many and so divine, although he worked much more by words than by deeds, his name and fame can never be extinguished; wherefore it was thus said in his praise by Messer Giovan Battista Strozzi: Vince costui pur solo / Tutti altri; e vince Fidia e vince Apelle / E tutto il lor vittorioso stuolo" (p. 640). The poem makes a pun between the name *Vinci* and the word *vince*, meaning "vanquishes": Vinci alone vanquishes all the others; and he vanquishes Pheidias and he vanquishes Apelles, and their whole victorious band.

And can we forget the words with which Vasari introduced his *Life* of "Lionardo da Vinci: Painter and Sculptor of Florence"? In the colorful language of which he was so fond, he summarized the salient characteristics of the man and the artist, "predicting" a future full of praise that in reality was already happening in his own time: "The greatest gifts are often seen, in the course of nature, rained by celestial influences on human creatures; and sometimes, in supernatural fashion, beauty, grace, and talent are united beyond measure in one single person, in a manner that to whatever such a one turns his attention, his every action is so divine, that, surpassing all other men, it makes itself clearly known as a thing bestowed by God (as it is), and not acquired by human art. This was seen by all mankind in Leonardo da Vinci, in whom, besides a beauty of body never sufficiently extolled, there was an infinite grace in all his actions; and so great was his genius, and such its growth, that to whatever difficulties he turned his mind, he solved them with ease. In him was great bodily strength, joined to dexterity, with a spirit and courage ever royal and magnanimous; and the fame of his name so increased, that not only in his lifetime was he held in esteem, but his reputation became even greater among posterity after his death" (p. 625). These words, written in 1550 (the second edition of the *Lives* appeared in 1568), are typical of Vasarian analysis, subjective, centered on Tuscan art, and viewing art history as an evolution toward perfection, which in his view was soon to arrive with Raphael and Michelangelo. But can we disagree with the historian's emphatic proclamation of the excellence of the man and the artist? An excellence that, according to Vasari, "became even greater among posterity after his death," so much so that Benedetto Varchi, in his public funeral oration for Michelangelo, who died in 1564, inserted an enumeration of the many talents of Leonardo, a rather strange thing to do on such an occasion.

The innumerable documents praising the art of Leonardo that followed in the course of the sixteenth, seventeenth, and eighteenth centuries make fascinating reading, reflecting, as they do, the tastes and intellectual trends of their eras. Despite the variations in focus, they never cast any doubt upon the quality of the artist's work, but instead underscore the perfect balance between

Previous pages:
Leonardo da Vinci
Five Grotesque Heads
ca. 1494
Pen and ink on paper
10.24 x 8.07 inches
(26 x 20.5 cm)
Royal Library, Windsor

Opposite:
Leonardo da Vinci
**Studies of
Central-Plan Buildings**
Pen and ink on paper
9.06 x 6.3 inches
(23 x 16 cm)
Bibliothèque de
l'Institut de France, Paris

his extraordinary pictorial skill and his intellectual breadth. Even Galileo was fascinated by Leonardo's numerous studies of the laws of the physics of flight and the mysteries of the universe.

In the nineteenth century, Johann Wolfgang von Goethe described the "universal" character of Leonardo's genius: "He never gave in to the latest impulse of his own original, matchless talent and restraining every spontaneous and casual impulse, wanted every part of a work to be meditated and remeditated." From the great German poet and writer comes a famous description of *The Last Supper*, in which he seeks to re-create the painting in words, in the manner of his time. The French critic Théophile Gautier did something similar in 1857, writing in the Parisian journal *L'Artiste* this description of the figures that populate Leonardo's paintings: "They seem to know that which men do not know, one would say that they have dwelt in more elevated and unknown territories before they came to shine on the linen canvas; their gazes are so mysterious, profound, penetrating, and wise, that while they delight, they also disturb, and at the same time they generate both love and fear." The poet Charles Baudelaire in *Les Fleurs du mal* (*Flowers of Evil*, 1857) and the painter Eugène Delacroix in the *Journal* (1857–1863) continued to enrich the romantic aura that colored the myth of the Tuscan artist with new poetic, evocative nuances. Baudelaire included Leonardo in his poem "The Beacons":

> Leonardo da Vinci, mirror deep and somber,
> Within which charming angels, with a sweet smile,
> Filled with mystery, appear in the shadow
> Of the glaciers and pines that enclose their land . . .

Vasari had seen Leonardo as having a few imperfections; the only peerless, unflawed artists, in his estimation, were Raphael and Michelangelo. But Hippolyte Taine, in *Voyage en Italie* (*Voyage to Italy*, 1866), praised the undisputed superiority of the painter from Vinci: "There is not in the world an example of genius more universal, inventive, incapable of being content, infinitely eager and naturally refined, stretching out beyond his own century and those that followed. . . . Next to his figures those of Michelangelo are mere heroic athletes; the virgins of Raphael are just placid girls whose sleepy soul has never lived. But his feel and think with every feature of their faces and bodies . . . " The nineteenth century, with its double interpretation of culture, at once romantic and positivist, kept the image of the genius alive, celebrating him as both the greatest affirmation of the uniqueness of the individual and a precursor of the Enlightenment's rationalist faith in human progress. And, of course, the most important art historians at the

Leonardo da Vinci
**Manuscript on
the Flight of Birds**
ca. 1505
Ink on paper
8.27 x 5.91 inches
(21 x 15 cm)
Royal Library, Turin

172

end of the century weighed in with thoughts on Leonardo: Bernard Berenson wrote that "Leonardo is the one artist of whom it may be said with perfect literalness: Nothing that he touched but turned into a thing of eternal beauty" (1896). Heinrich Wölfflin noted that "For Leonardo, the painter is like a clear eye that surveys the world and takes all visible things for its domain." (1899).

In the course of the myriad critiques of his art, increasing space was given to personal and subjective analysis and questions focused on purely human issues concerning the painter. The early twentieth century was the golden age for coming up with satisfying answers to all such questions, since intellectual attention was turned, in these decades, almost entirely to the exploration of the interior life of the individual. A personality such as Leonardo, whose thought was impenetrable, came to symbolize an enigmatic and mysterious nature, into which interpreters poured every sort of fantasy. The father of psychoanalysis, Sigmund Freud, was fascinated by him and in 1910 devoted an essay to interpreting his genius; the plausibility of Freud's conclusions is debatable, but the text offers evidence of the continuing allure of the artist well into the modern era. Freud analyzed the artist's works and working method based on his childhood experiences and what he knew of Leonardo's relationship with his father.

The 1900s marked the birth of the modern scientific method in art history: archives were opened and documentary sources mined and collated, permitting interpretations to be based on facts. The manuscripts and drawings of Leonardo now began to be published, allowing the artist and his work to be understood in a more unified and contextual manner. New biographies appeared, rigorously founded on documentary sources, although it was 1998 before the immense project of publishing Leonardo's complete "Codices" in facsimile came to fruition.

Each of Leonardo's paintings, studies, and drawings has always attracted interest, which has only grown with time, but *The Last Supper* and the *Mona Lisa* are without a doubt the most popular works and hold a place of pride in the canon. Indeed, some claim that the Leonardo myth revolves entirely around these two works, among the most famous paintings in the history of art. With the passage of the centuries, tastes and theories have changed, linked to various trends and currents of thought; new interpretations have been added to old, and numerous new ideas have been attached to every minute detail of these iconic works. If many artists in the fifteenth century were already occupied in attempting more or less faithful reproductions of Leonardo's oeuvre, by the nineteenth century, and even more in the twentieth, *The Last Supper* and the *Mona Lisa* took center stage. The latter in particular became a sort of obsession, a fetish, a symbol of Art with a capital A, and therefore an

Jean-Baptiste-Camille Corot
Lady with a Pearl
1868–1870
Musée du Louvre, Paris

object of actual veneration, as well as a victim of desecration and attacks. This oscillation is endemic in art history, where the alternation of critical positions between two opposing perspectives is the rule rather than the exception. In the case of the *Mona Lisa*, this holds even more true, given the immediate acclaim with which it was received even in Leonardo's own lifetime. The painting was clothed in so overly luminous an aura that it could not pass unobserved by artists of later centuries. When the painting was taken from Italy to France by Napoleon in 1800, residing first in his bedroom at the Tuileries and then in the Louvre in 1804, this ratified it as the icon of an artist and a century. The *Mona Lisa* was the inspiration for many painters, beginning with Jean-Baptiste-Camille Corot, who, for his *Lady with a Pearl* of 1868–1870 (Musée du Louvre, Paris), borrowed the sitter's pose from Leonardo's panel, including the slight torsion of her bust and the hands folded at her waist. Nor was there any lack of mythifications of this most enigmatic of paintings in the literature of the time: from Georges Sand to Jules Laforgue, from Walter Pater to Oscar Wilde, and from Jules Verne to Gabriele D'Annunzio, the nineteenth century was rich in literary treatments of it.

With the arrival of the avant-garde in the first fifteen years of the twentieth century, celebration of the painting turned to defamation in the general climate of

Kazimir Malevich
Partial Eclipse of the Sun with Mona Lisa
1914
State Russian Museum, St. Petersburg

modernization and transformation of the world. In particular the Futurists, led by F. T. Marinetti, exalted the modern as a symbol of human progress and rejected all that was traditional and academic. It was therefore almost inevitable that all those venerable icons of the past, which had for generations been treated as ideal models and sources of valuable instruction, should fall from grace. The words of the Futurist Ardengo Soffici may be understood in this context: "I see written on a wall in big white letters on a blue ground: GIOCONDA ACQUA PURA ITALIANA [Mona Lisa Pure Italian Water]. And below it the buttery face of Mona Lisa. Finally! See, even here we can become good art critics." Carlo Carrà, another member of the Italian Futurists, called Leonardo's masterpiece "fetid." None of this should be understood as an attempt to destroy Leonardo's artistic reputation, but as a declaration embracing modernity, which must look only forward and construct the world *ex novo*, without looking backward to the past.

The exaltations of and attacks on the *Mona Lisa* turned up in both critical commentaries and actual artworks. For example, in 1914 the father of Suprematism, the Russian painter Kazimir Malevich, painted *Partial Eclipse of the Sun with Mona Lisa* (State Russian Museum, St. Petersburg) and symbolically erased the iconic image by marking a reproduction of it with two red Xs. A well-known reworking of the painting is Marcel Duchamp's

L.H.O.O.Q. of 1919, commonly known as the *Mona Lisa with a Mustache* (Private Collection). With this work a major protagonist of the Dada movement, which began in New York between 1915 and 1917, created the archetype of any future transgressive image of Leonardo's painting. Although Duchamp modified the *Mona Lisa* with only a minimal intervention in a reproduction of the original work, he managed effortlessly to invert the entire meaning of it, and to turn it into an emblem of Dada ideology. This was possible above all through the introduction of the intentionally provocative title, whose initials, when pronounced in French, sound like "*Elle a chaud au cul* (Her ass is burning)."

In contrast to the Futurists, Duchamp wanted to demonstrate that the fundamental element in a work of art is the idea, and therefore the title: Any material object can be elevated to the status of art if the artist confers a sense of value on it. By this road Duchamp arrived at the idea of the famous Readymades, ordinary objects removed from their normal context, stripped of their usual function, and transformed into works of art. It is the idea itself that confirms their renewed aesthetic value.

The Spanish Surrealist artist Salvador Dalí also added a mustache to the face of the *Mona Lisa in Self-Portrait as the Mona Lisa* of 1954 (Fundación Gala-Salvador Dalí, Figueras); in this case the mustache matches the artist's own famous one, creating an ironic ambivalence of meaning that in its own way draws upon the new modes of interpretation offered by Freudian analysis. In 1930 Fernand Léger painted *Mona Lisa with the Keys* (Musée National Fernand Léger, Biot), in which Leonardo's image is placed together with mechanical shapes and objects typical of this proponent of Orphic Cubism (a "heretical" branch of Cubism, so defined by the French critic Guillaume Apollinaire), who was interested in industrial society and the workers' world.

Every element of the past is absorbed into modernity, reconsidered according to the point of view of the moment, and stripped of prior meanings. Many other artists have continued to make use of the *Mona Lisa*, reconfiguring or reworking it. Despite the tendency to ironize and deface it, they bear witness to its unquestioned immortality, to the fact that it has become an irrefutable point of reference. In this context we may recall Andy Warhol's *Mona Lisa* of 1963, at the height of the Pop Art movement. The repetition of the work becomes emblematic of a meditation on the communicative power of images. Conscious that contemporary viewers are decreasingly able to establish relationships, the American artist realized that even the most powerful images lose their force over time and become drained of meaning. His work deals with the concept of repetition, a fundamental aspect of the new era of mass communications and mass media, and with the appropriation of images, that at one time stood at the

Right:
Marcel Duchamp
L.H.O.O.Q.
1919
Private Collection

Following pages:
Andy Warhol
Mona Lisa
1963
Andy Warhol Foundation,
New York

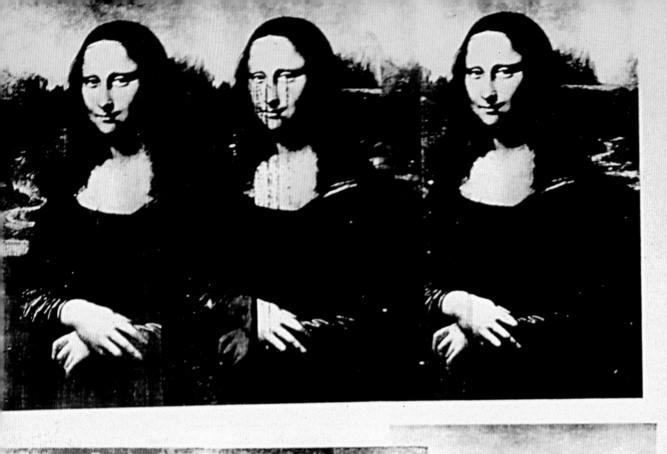

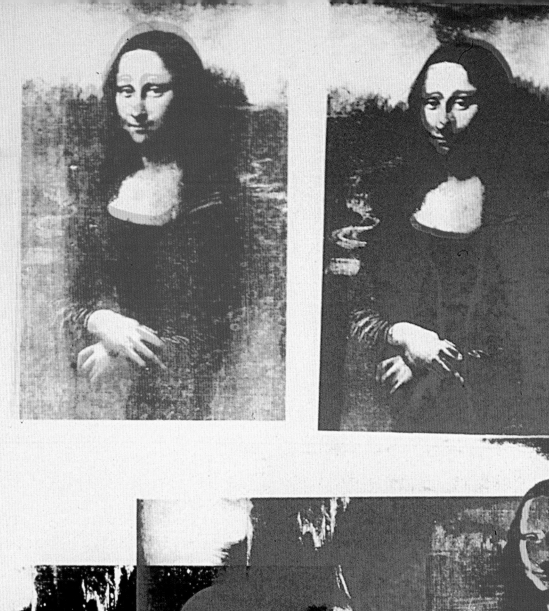

apex of culture. The meaning lies in understanding that the repetition of the same subject leads quickly to its "death," that is, to the loss of its uniqueness of meaning. The artistic act remains the sole means of intervening to arrest this swift obsolescence.

The Last Supper has suffered a similar fate, object of both panegyrics and condemnations, of copies and reworkings—proving once more that one cannot cross Leonardo's path without being struck and fascinated. It was again Andy Warhol who gave form to a new interpretation of the work, with his *Last Supper* of 1986 (Andy Warhol Foundation, New York), made when the fresco itself was closed to the public for conservation. His version was born of the desire to render an icon of international culture recognizable through its reproduction—not aiming to maintain the qualitative value of the original, but rather to cite its notoriety and immediate recognizability. For this reason he decided to work from a reproduction of the painting rather than the original, selecting a photographic print of a nineteenth-century copy by Giuseppe Bossi. Warhol made several versions on paper, canvas, and in screenprint, and then reproduced them photographically using various colored grounds and, in other

Above and right:
Andy Warhol
The Last Supper
1986
Andy Warhol Foundation,
New York

instances, overprinting with images taken from the media world. The result comprises about one hundred variations on the theme of *The Last Supper* of Leonardo.

Over time, the collective imagination has accumulated a visual sampler of historical works, often without noticing the process of decontextualization imposed on them by the medium of mass communications. We need only think of Leonardo's *Vitruvian Man* (Accademia, Venice), the 1490 drawing in which he studied human proportions, inscribing the figure in a circle and a square. Most, if not all of us, are so used to this image, and meet it so often, in the oddest contexts, that its true value and its artistic and historical meaning are lost. It too has been "redone" many times. In 1987 the sculptor Mario Ceroli turned the drawing into a large three-dimensional sculpture that stands in the piazza before the Museum of Leonardo in Vinci. Not long ago the same image was stamped onto the 1-euro coins of the new European currency.

As we conclude this survey of the critical vicissitudes of the Leonardo myth, we should mention the ways in which popular culture, too, has celebrated this genius, with particular attention to his personality and his human dimension. In 1950 the film *The Last Supper*, directed by Luigi Giachino, appeared, and in 1984, the absurd and brilliant comedy *Nothing Left to Do But Cry* (*Non ci resta che piangere*), with the inimitable Roberto Benigni and Massimo Troisi, introduced an ironic version of the painter. The most recent example of popular culture drawing on Leonardo's name and fame is *The Da Vinci Code*, the bestselling novel by Dan Brown, which was made into a feature film directed by Tom Hanks. The story took as its springboard Leonardo's love of codemaking, another aspect of his genius, his boundless curiosity, and his mischievous nature. *The Da Vinci Code* has exposed a whole new audience to Leonardo and his art, and has ensured that his legacy will endure in the collective memory.

What the great master of Vinci has left us is an immense patrimony of studies, observations, and intuitions in addition to his inestimably precious works of art. We should not, however, discount another aspect of his experience as a man and an artist that has come down to us and that will always have the greatest value: the capacity to open our eyes to the world; the desire to investigate every minute aspect of the reality that surrounds us and not to dismiss anything as insignificant; and the awareness, which we must always keep in mind and at heart, that we are all part of one unique, extraordinary "little planet."

Leonardo da Vinci
Vitruvian Man
1490
Pen, ink, and brush on paper
13.5 x 9.65 inches
(34.3 x 24.5 cm)
Accademia, Venice

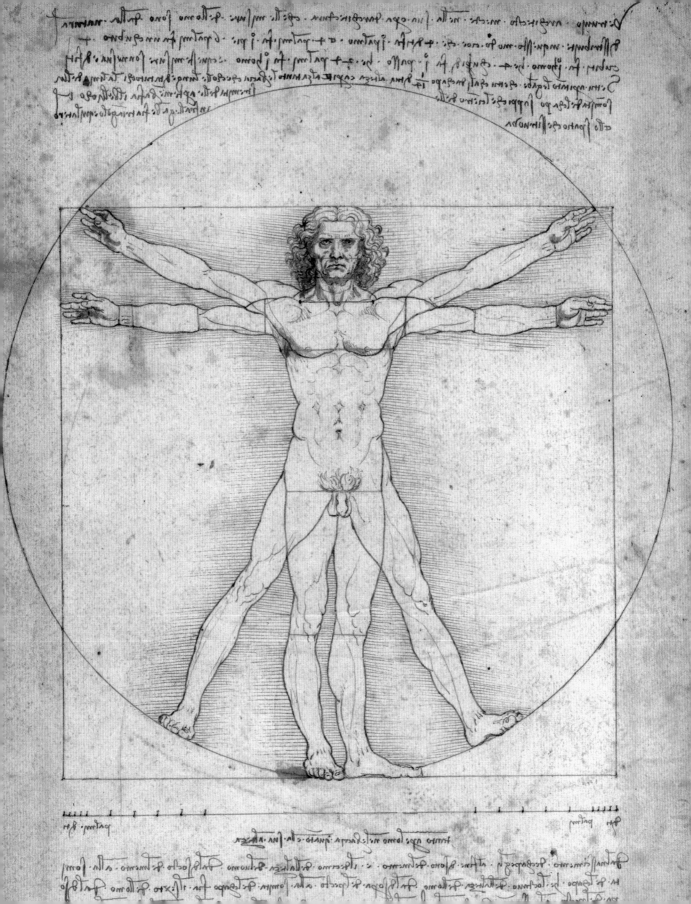

Index

Page numbers in *italics* indicate illustrations. All works are by Leonardo unless otherwise indicated.

A

Adoration of the Magi, 42, *43*, 46
  commissioning of, 38
  detail, *44–45*
  inception of, 20
  study for, *38*, *46*, *47*
Albertini, Francesco, 26, 111
Alexander VI, Pope, 97
Amadori, Albiera degli, 5
Amboise, Charles d'
  in Leonardo's move to Florence, 131
  and Leonardo's return to Milan, 122
  villa of, 132
Anchiano (town), 5
Andrea, Giovanni di, 108
Anghiari, Battle of, 107
The Annunciation, 28–29, 30–31, *30–31*
  attribution of, 22
  cloth folds in, 18
  detail, *4*, *32–33*, 34
Annunzio, Gabriele D', 176
Apollinaire, Guillaume, 178
architecture, 132
Arte dei Mercanti, 6

B

Bacchus, 161
  detail, *162–163*
Saint John the Baptist and, 156
  study for, *160*
Baptism of Christ (Leonardo, Verrochio), 26, *26*, 27
Vasari on, 20
Battle of Anghiari, 107
Battle of Anghiari
  fate of, 110–111
  inspiration for, 107
  integration in, 122
  Leda and, 132, 136
  study for, *112*, *114–115*
  Vasari on, 112
Battle of Cascina, 108
Battle of Cascina (Sangallo), *110*
Baudelaire, Charles, 172
Bazzi, Giovanni
  reconstructions of, 120

work of, *123*, *124*, *125*
Beatis, Antonio de, 126
Bellincioni, Bernardo, 168
Bellini, Giovanni, 12, 64
Bembo, Bernardo, 20
Benci, Amerigo, 20
Benci, Ginevra, 20, 60
Benigni, Roberto, 184
Benois Madonna, 36, *37*
Berenson, Bernard, 174
Boltraffio, Antonio, 88, 136, 148
Bonfire of the Vanities, 98
Borgia, Cesare, 106, *106*
Botticelli, Sandro
  and *Baptism of Christ*, 26
  in Florentine history, 29
  stylistic shift in, 99–100
Verrocchio and, 10
Brandano, Pacifica, 126
Brown, Dan, 184
Brunelleschi, Filippo, *11*, 11–12, 29

C

Carrà, Carlo, 177
Cartoon for Virgin and Child with Saint Anne and the Young Saint John the Baptist, 103, *104–105*
Cascina, Battle of, 108
Cathedral of Pistoia, 22
Cellini, Benevenuto, 108, 111
Ceroli, Mario, 184
Chapel of St. Bernardo, 22
chiaroscuro, 12, 31
Chronicles (Dei), 7
Church of San Bartolomeo, 30–31
Church of San Donato a Scopeto, 42
Church of San Lorenzo, 30
Church of San Salvi, 20
Church of the Santissima Annunziata, 101
Cliffs with Water Birds, 59
Clouet, Jean, *165*
Cloux chateau, *164*
Colleoni Monument (Verrochio), 22
Confraternity of the Immaculate Conception, 52
Corot, Jean-Baptiste-Camille, *175*, 176
Cortigiani, Lucrezia di Guglielmo, 5
Cosimo, Piero di, 29
Cosimo il Vecchio, 22, 28

Credi, Lorenzo di
  and Cathedral of Pistoia, 22
  chiaroscuro by, 12
  at Garden of San Marco, 28
  and Savonarola, 98
Verrocchio and, 10
Crivelli, Lucrezia, 62
Cronaca rimata (Rhymed chronicle) (Santi), 6
Cubism, 178

D

Da Vinci Code (novel, film), 184
Dada, 178
Dalí, Salvador, 178
David (Michelangelo), 108, *111*
De divina proportione (On Divine Proportion) (Pacioli), 72
Dei, Benedetto, 7
Delacroix, Eugène, 172
Deluge drawings, 164
del Vacca, Antonio di Piero Buti, 5
del Vacca, Caterina, 5
Donatello, 28
Doni, Anton Francesco, 111
Doubting Thomas group (Verrocchio), 16
Dreyfus Madonna. See Madonna and Child with a Pomegranate (The Dreyfus Madonna) (attrib.)
Duchamp, Marcel, 177–178, *179*

E

Este, Beatrice d', 50, *93*
Este, Isabella d', *92*
  family of, 88
  Lady with an Ermine and, 64
  Madonna and Child with a Yarn Winder and, 144
  Mona Lisa and, 126
  Novellara and, 101
Este family, 49
Execution of Savarola (attrib. Rosselli), 98
Eyck, Jan van, 29

F

Feast of Paradise, 168
Ficino, Marsilio, 28
Fight for the Standard. See also Battle of Anghiari

copies of, 114, *118–119*
evidence for, 111
range in, 120
film, 184
Fiorentino, Rosso, 122
Five Grotesque Heads, 168–169
Fleurs du Mal (Flowers of Evil)
(Baudelaire), 172
Florence
Leonardo's father as notary of, 6
workshops in, 7
Florence Cathedral, *11*, 11–12
Fontebuoni, Anastasio, *100*
fresco, 108, 110
Freud, Sigmund, 174
Futurism, 177

G
Gaddiano, Anonimo, 28
Gaffurio, Franchino, 60
Galileo, 172
Gallerani, Cecilia, 62, 64, 88
Garden of San Marco, 28
Gautier, Théophile, 172
Gherardini, Lisa, 126
Ghirlandaio, Domenico, 10, 29
Giachino, Luigi, 184
Giocondo, Francesco del, 126
Giovanni, Bertoldo di, 10, *10*, 28
Goes, Hugo van der, 29, *36*
Goethe, Johann Wolfgang von, 172
gold ground, 98
Granacci, Francesco, 28
Gualanda, Isabella, 126
Guicciardini, Francesco, 22
Guild of Saint Luke, 11

H
Head of a Woman, 48
Head of a Young Girl, 96
Head of Leda, 120
Holy Family (Luini), 102

I
Isabella of Aragon, 62, 168

J
Jacopo, Margherita di Francesco, 5

L
La Belle Ferronière, 62, 69
Lady of Cracow, 62
Lady with a Bunch of Flowers
(Verrocchio), 16, *20*
Lady with a Pearl (Corot), *175*, 176
Lady with an Ermine, 64, 65

d'Este and, 88
detail, *66–67*
formality in, 92
Gallernani and, 64
as "motions of the mind"
paradigm, 62
Laforgue, Jules, 176
Lamentation over the Dead Christ
(Botticelli), 99, *99*
Lanfredini, Francesca, 5
Lanfredini, Giuliano, 5
L'Artiste (journal), 172
The Last Supper, 70–71, 72
commissioning of, 68
detail, *73, 78–79, 81, 82–83*
Goethe and, 172
popularity of, 174
psychology in, 64
study for, *72, 74–75, 76–77*
through time, *182,* 184
Vasari on, 68
Last Supper (film), 184
Last Supper (Warhol), *182, 183,* 184
Leda, 18, 107, 120, 132, 136
Leda (Bazzi), *123, 124, 125*
Leda (Peruzzi), 144
Leda (Sesto), 144, *145, 146–147*
Léger, Fernand, *177,* 178
Leonardo da Vinci
birth of, 5
chiaroscuro of, 31
childhood of, 5–6
collaboration with Verrocchio, 16
family of, 5, 6, 108
in Milan, 49–50, 52
varied interests of, 11
*Leonardo Describes His Artistic and
Mechanical Inventions to Ludovico
Sforza* (Cianfanelli), *50*
L.H.O.O.Q (Duchamp), 177–178,
179
Lippi, Filippino
Adoration of the Magi and, 42
gold ground use of, 98
Nunziata and, 101
at Pollaiolo workshop, 29
pregnancy imagery and, 31
Lollio, Alberto, 111
Lomazzo, Gian Paolo, 120
Louis XII, 50
Luini, Bernardino, 102, 136

M
Machiavelli, Niccolò, 100, 108
Madonna and Child with Angels
(attrib. Verrocchio), 16, *17*

*Madonna and Child with a
Pomegranate (The Dreyfus
Madonna)* (attrib.), *13*, 16
Adoration of the Magi and, 20
attribution of, 12
detail, *14–15*
Madonna of the Carnation and, 18
*Madonna and Child with a Yarn-
Winder* (attrib.), 144, *149*
*Madonna and Child with a Yarn-
Winder* (School of Leonardo),
150, 151
Madonna di Piazza (Verrochio), 22,
30
Madonna Lita, 88, *89, 90–91*
Madonna of the Carnation, 18, *21,*
23
Madonna of the Cat, 61
Madonna of the Flower, 36, *37*
Madonna of the Little Trees (Bellini),
12
Maino, Giacomo del, 54
Malevich, Kazimir, *176,* 177
Manuscript on the Flight of Birds, 173
Martelli, Piero di Braccio, 101, 122
Maximilian (Holy Roman Emperor),
49
*Medal with the Oath of the Pazzi
and a Portrait of Giuliano de'
Medici* (Giovanni), *10*
Medici, Giovanni de', 30
Medici, Giuliano de', 152, 156
Medici, Lorenzo de'
collection of, 28
death of, 96
in Florentine government, 22
Sforza and, 49
Medici, Piero de', 22, 28, 30
Medici family, 6
Medici tomb, 30
Melzi, Francesco, 165
Memling, Hans, 29
Messina, Anotello da, 35, 60
Michelangelo, *100*
commissioned by Florentine
government, 108
flees Florence, 100
frescoes of, *155*
Giovanni and, 28
in Renaissance, 152
Vasari on, 172
vs. Leonardo, 120
*Michelangelo Presents Himself to
Julius II in Bologna* (Fontebuoni),
100
Milan, 49–50, 131

Mirandola, Pico della, 28
Mona Lisa, 126, *127*, 128
    Leonardo starts, 107
    dating of, 122
    detail, *129*
    popularity of, 174
    Portrait of Isabella d'Este and, 92
    through time, 176–178
*Mona Lisa in Self-Portrait as the
    Mona Lisa* (Dalí), 178
Mona Lisa (Warhol), 178, *180–181*
*Mona Lisa with a Moustache. See
    L.H.O.O.Q* (Duchamp)
Mona Lisa with the Keys (Léger),
    177, 178
Montefeltro family, 49
Montefeltro, Frederico da, 6
music, 122
The Musician, 60, 62, *63*
Mystic Nativity (Botticelli), 99–100

N
naturalism, 38
*Nothing Left to Do But Cry (Non ci
    resta che piangere)* (film), 184
Novellara, Pietro da, 101–102, 144

O
Oggiono, Marco d', 136, 148
oil painting, 35
Orsini, Piergiampaolo, 107

P
Pacioli, Luca, 72
Palazzo Vecchio, 22
Pallanti, Giuseppe, 126
*Partial Eclipse of the Sun with Mona
    Lisa* (Malevich), *176*, 177
Pater, Walter, 176
*Perspective Study for the Background
    of The Adoration of the Magi, 40–41*
Perugino, Piero, 6, 10, 98
Peruzzi, Baldasare, 144
Piccinino, Francesco, 107
Piccinino, Niccolò, 107
Platonic Academy, 28
Pollaiolo workshop, 28
Pontormo, 122
Porta, Bartolomeo della, 100
Portinari Triptych (Goes), *36*
Portrait of a Lady, 62, *69*
Portrait of Beatrice d'Este (Predis), *93*
Portrait of Cesare Borgia (anon.), *106*
Portrait of Francis I, King of France
    (Clouet), *165*
Portrait of Ginevra de' Benci, 18, 20,

24, 25, 60
Portrait of Isabella d'Este, 92, *92*
Portrait of Louis XII King of France
    (Altissimo), *94*
Portrait of Maddalena Doni
    (Raphael), 126, *126*
Portrait of Niccolò Macchiavelli
    (Tito), *101*
portraiture, 60, 64
Predis, Ambrogio de', 54, *93*, 136
Predis, Evangelista de', 54
Prèz, Josquin des, 60

R
Raphael
    Leonardo and, 144
    father of, 6
    fresoes of, *154*
    influence of, 122
    Mona Lisa and, 126
    Vatican and, 152
Reformation, 152
Rhymes (Bellincioni), 168, 170
Rome, 106
Romorantin chateau, 164
Rubens, Peter Paul, 120
Rustici, Giovan Francesco, 28, 122

S
*Saint Anne, the Virgin, and Child
    with the Lamb*, 138, *139*
    detail, *140–141, 142–143*
    return to Milan and, 136
    study for, *137, 138*
    Vasari and, 100
    Vasari on, 101–102
Saint Jerome, 38, *39*
Saint John the Baptist, 152, 156,
    157, 158–159
Sala delle Asse (Chamber of the Wood
    Panels), 68, *84, 85, 86–87*
Salai, 136, 165
Sand, Georges, 176
Sangallo, Bastiano da, *110*
Sansovino, 28
Santa Maria delle Grazie, 68, 72
Santi, Giovanni, 6
Sarto, Andrea del, 122
Savonarola, Girolamo, 97–99
Scarampo, Ludovico, 107
Scotti, Giovanni, 152
Self-Portrait, 166
Sesto, Cesare da
    Leda and, 136, 144, *145, 146–147*
    style of, Leonardo and, 136, 144
Sforza, Francesco, 5

Sforza, Gian Galeazzo, 168
Sforza, Ludovico
    ascendance of, 49
    Crivelli and, 62
    Leonardo presents himself to, 50
    Leonardo summoned by, 52
    Last Supper and, 72
    Sala delle Asse and, 68
    Virgin of the Rocks and, 54
Sforza monument, 52, *53*
sfumato shading, 16, 168
Sistine Chapel, *155*
Sketch for the Madonna of the Cat, 61
Sketch of the Arno Valley, 8–9, 16
Soderini, Pier, 100, 108, 131
Sodoma, il, 144
Soffici, Ardengo, 177
Solario, Andrea, 136
Stanza della Segnatura, *154*
*Star of Bethlehem, Wood Anemone
    and Sun Splurge (Study for Leda),
    58*
Strozzi, Giovan Battista, 170
Studies of Central-Plan Buildings, 171
Study for a Flying Machine, 95
Study for Saint Anne, 138
*Study for Saint Anne, the Virgin,
    and Child with the Lamb, 137*
Study for the Battle of Cascina
    (Michelangelo), *106, 109*
*Study for the compositional plan of
    The Last Supper, 72*
*Study for the Head of James the
    Greater, 80*
Study for the Head of Leda, 122
*Study for the Head of Saint
    Bartholomew, 77*
*Study for the Heads for the Battle
    of Anghiari, 112–113*
Study for the Last Supper, 74–75
Study for the Sforza Monument, 53
*Study for the Trivulzio Monument,
    133, 134–135*
Study of a Dragon, 18
Study of a Rearing Horse, 121
*Study of Combatants on Horseback
    and on Foot for the Battle of
    Anghiari, 114–115, 116–117*
*Study with Madonna Nursing and
    Profile Heads, 88*

T
Taine, Hippolyte, 172
Tito, Santi di, *101*
Tobias and the Angel (attrib.
    Verrocchio), 16, *19*

Tornabuoni, Lucrezia, 22
Torre, Marcantonio della, 133
Torrigiano, Pietro, 28
Treatise on Painting, 18, 26, 112, 122, 167–168
Trivulzio, Gian Giacomo, 131
Trivulzio monument, 131–132, *133, 134–135*
Troisi, Massimo, 184

V
Vasari, Giorgio
    on *Adoration of the Magi*, 42
    on *Baptism of Christ*, 20
    on *Battle of Anghiari*, 112
    on chiaroscuro, 31
    on Leonardo, 170
    on Leonardo in Milan, 50, 52
    on Leonardo's varied interests, 11
    as first art historian, 6
    and Garden of San Marco, 28
    on *Last Supper*, 68
    on Ludovico monument, 52
    on Verrocchio, 20

on Verrocchio's introduction to Leonardo, 6–7
Verne, Jules, 176
Verrocchio, Andrea del
    and *The Annunciation*, 30
    and *Baptism of Christ*, 26
    collaboration with Leonardo, 16
    introduction to Leonardo, 6–7
    Madonna and Child with Angels and, 16
    Madonna di Piazza and, 22
    Medici tomb and, 30
        and Santa Maria del Fiore cupola, 11–12
    sculpture of, 12, *20*
    Vasari on, 20
    workshop of, 6
Vinci (town), 5
Virgin and Child with Saint Anne and the Young Saint John the Baptist, 102, *103, 104–105*
Virgin of the Rocks (First Version), 54, 55, *56–57*
Virgin of the Rocks (Second Version),

130, 148, *153*
Visconti, Francesco Maria, 107
Vite delle più eccelenti pittori, scultori, ed architettori, Le (Lives of the Most Excellent Painters, Sculptors, and Architects) (Vasari), 6–7
Vitruvian Man, 184, *185*
Voyage en Italie (Voyage to Italy) (Taine), 172

W
Warhol, Andy, 178, *180–181, 183*, 184
Wilde, Oscar, 176
Wölfflin, Heinrich, 174

Y
Young Bacchus, 160

Further Reading

Bambach, Carmen, et al. *Leonardo da Vinci: Master Draftsman*, exh. cat., New York: Metropolitan Museum of Art, 2003

Barcilon, Pinin Brambilla and Pietro C. Marani. *Leonardo: The Last Supper*, translated by Harlow Tighe, Chicago: University of Chicago Press, 2001.

Bramly, Serge. *Leonardo: The Artist and the Man*, translated by Sian Reynolds, New York: HarperCollins, 1991.

Brown, David Alan. *Leonardo da Vinci: Origins of a Genius*, New Haven: Yale University Press, 1998.

Clark, Kenneth. *Leonardo da Vinci*, 1939, revised and edited by Martin Kemp, London: Penguin, 1993.

Farrago, Claire ed. *Leonardo's Writings and Theory of Art*, 5 vols., London: Garland, 1999.

Kemp, Martin. *Leonardo da Vinci: The Marvellous Works of Nature and Man*, revised edition, Oxford: Oxford University Press, 2006.

———. *Leonardo*, Oxford: Oxford University Press, 2004.

———, ed. *Leonardo on Painting*, translated by Martin Kemp and Margaret Walker, New Haven: Yale University Press, 1989.

Marani, Pietro C. *Leonardo da Vinci*, New York: Abrams, 2003.

McCurdy, J. *The Notebooks of Leonardo da Vinci*, 2 vols., London: Reynal and Hitchcock, 1938.

Popham, A.E., ed. *The Journals of Leonardo da Vinci*, London: Pimlico, Random House, 1994.

Richter, Jean Paul. *The Literary Works of Leonardo da Vinci, 2 vols.* Oxford: Dover, 1970.

Steinberg, Leo. *Leonardo's Incessant Last Supper*, New York: Zone, 2001.

Vasari, Giorgio. "Leonardo da Vinci," in *Lives of the Painters, Sculptors, and Architects*, translated by Gaston du C. de Vere, vol. 1, New York: Everyman's Library, Knopf, 1927, 1996.

Image Credits

The illustrations in this volume were supplied by the Scala Archive, the most prestigious fine art archive in the world. The more than 60,000 subjects are accessible through a computerized system that permits easy, quick iconographic research of any degree of complexity. Website: *www.scalarchives.it*; e-mail: *archivio@scalagroup.it*.

Other images supplied by:

pp. 13, 14–15 Washington, D.C., National Gallery of Art, Samuel H. Kress Collection. Photo: ©Board of Trustees National Gallery of Art, Washington, D.C.
p. 17 London, National Gallery
p. 18 Windsor, Windsor Castle. Photo: ©Her Majesty Queen Elizabeth II
p. 19 London, National Gallery
pp. 21, 23 Munich, Bayerische Staatsgemäldesammlungen, Alte Pinakothek
pp. 24, 25 Washington, D.C., Ailsa Mellon Bruce Foundation. Photograph ©Board of Trustees National Gallery of Art, Washington, D.C.
pp. 84–85, 86–87 Milan, Museo Civico d'Arte Antica, Sala delle Asse, Castello Sforzesco. Photo: Foto Saporetti
p. 96 Parma, Galleria Nazionale, Archivio Fotografico Soprintendenza per il Patrimonio Storico, Artistico e

Demoetnoantropologico (PSAD) di Parma e Piacenza. Photo: Galloni e Medioli. By permission of the Ministero per i Beni e le Attività Culturali
pp. 103, 104–5 London, National Gallery
p. 130 London, National Gallery
p. 149 New York, private collection. Photo provided by Museum Ideale Leonardo da Vinci (LDV)
p. 150 Thornhill, Collection of the Duke of Buccleuch and Queensberry, KT
p. 153 London, National Gallery
p. 176 St. Petersburg, State Russian Museum/Bridgeman/Alinari
p. 177 Biot, Musée Fernand Léger, Photo: © éunion des Musées Nationaux/Gérard Blot
p. 179 Private Collection, New York. ©ARS, NY, L.H.O.O.Q., 1930. Photo: Cameraphoto/Art Resource, NY

© 2004 by Rusconi Libri

This 2007 edition published by Barnes & Noble, Inc.

ISBN-13: 978-0-7607-8955-1
ISBN-10: 0-7607-8955-X

Printed and bound in China

1 3 5 7 9 10 8 6 4 2